THE TIME,
THE PLACE

Sarah Woods

NEW
HOLLAND

Introduction

The genesis of 'The Time, The Place' concept came as I was daydreaming at my desk. I wondered what was going on in other parts of the world. What was happening at this point in time in New York City, Benin, Panama, or, for that matter, Lithuania? By spending that particular day at work I might be missing out on the opportunity to experience a unique event somewhere else in the world. Such a chance could be lost forever, or at least for another year. How could I make sure that I never missed a life-changing travel experience or event again? A quick search of the web and bookshops revealed little definitive information on the subject. The usual major festivals and travel clichés were trotted out, but there was nothing that really addressed the question of where the most interesting place was to be at any given time and place.

The concept behind this book is simple – it is a travellers' guide to the most awe-inspiring, fun, unusual and interesting experiences to be had on each day of the year around the world. This is much more than a simple list of events and festivals. We cast our net wide and discover essential experiences in all sorts of categories: arts and culture, sports and adrenaline, gastronomy, music, the natural world, amazing landscapes, partying and many more. Some events, such as Mexican Independence Day, Harrod's winter sale in London and the Day of the Gaucho in Argentina, occur on exactly the same day each year and are listed under the appropriate date in the book. The dates of others, such as Mani Rimdu in Nepal, change every year according to the lunar cycle or another calendar. In such cases we have listed them within the appropriate range of dates and given further information on how to find out the exact date each year. Others, like the wildebeest migration in Tanzania and Kenya, are seasonal and occur at an approximate time each year. Finally, some activities, such as visiting the amazing souks of Sana'a in Yemen, can be done at any time of year, but we tell you the ultimate time to visit based on the weather, the availability of certain goods and a host of other factors.

All seven continents are well represented in this book, and the colour-coding system helps you to identify easily the continent that each experience occurs in. With a whole world of destinations, events and happenings and only 366 days (365 plus one for leap years) to fill, the main challenge in researching this book was what to leave out, rather than what to include. In the end, we came up with a simple set of questions to decide what to put in: is it fresh and exciting? Is it a definitive, one-of-a-kind event, the best in its class? And finally, is it absolutely the best place in the world to be on that day of the year?

Sure, there are lots of destinations and events in this book that will be familiar to many readers – the Rio Carnival is a prime example. We've included these events because despite their popularity and notoriety, they remain definitive world events that any self-respecting traveller should aspire to visit once in their lifetime. Others, such as Christmas day, are observed in many parts of the world and there are many interesting ways to spend the day. However, when we have listed a well- known event we've done so from a fresh or unusual angle. So, for example, for the Rio Carnival we recommend that you join a workshop at one of the carnival samba schools for an authentic backstage slice of the action, and we spend Christmas day in the serene setting of the Marshall Islands.

For every well-known event, you will find a host of more esoteric but equally fascinating places and downright cool things to do around the world. Ever wanted to go bog-snorkelling in Wales, moose-spotting in New Hampshire, sea-kayaking in Greenland or witness the yearly invasion of the Christmas Islands by legions of red crabs? All of these activities are described in the book along with many more innovative suggestions that will inspire the most jaded of travellers.

You can use this book in several different ways – you can scan the contents page for experiences that take your fancy and quickly dip into the book to discover more; you can read what's happening on any particular date or time of year to ensure you don't miss an essential event, or to plan fun things to do on your holiday; or finally you can read the book from cover to cover or dive in at random to marvel at the multitude of weird and wonderful things going on around the world at any one time. Whichever you choose, *The Time, The Place* will ensure that you never miss an essential travel experience again.

Contents

Key

- Africa
- Australia/Pacific
- Asia
- Europe
- North America
- South America

Contents

Contents

Contents

1 New Year's Day

Kiribati

The 33 atolls of Kiribati are mere pinpricks in the vast expanse of the Pacific Ocean where islanders live on coconuts, breadfruit and fish in mud-and-thatch huts just as they have done for centuries past. Yet the Republic of Kiribati (pronounced 'Kiri-bas') boasts a great claim to fame as the nation that straddles the equator – and is therefore the first nation on Earth to celebrate New Year's Day. Kiribati's capital Tarawa sits about half-way between Hawaii and Australia at GMT +12. A unilateral adjustment in 1995 enabled the entire country to keep to the same time zone.

📅 1st Jan (the first New Year's Day in the world)

ℹ Kiribati Tourism www.visit-kiribati.com

Straddle the equator to revel in the first new year in the world's time zones

2 Camel Wrestling

Selcuk, Turkey

Ancient Turkic tribes originated the spectacle of camel wrestling though, today, it owes more to comedy than sport. A succession of prized bull camels are paraded through Selcuk in elaborate saddles with golden bells on their humps, bejewelled blankets across their flanks and tails woven with colourful pompoms. Winter is the mating season – and the only time Turkey's camels tussle in order to win the right to available females.

Most settle for a half-hearted succession of butts and shoulder-to-shoulder nudges. Others rampage through the crowds, scattering 25,000 spectators across the makeshift arena in a frenzy of high excitement.

📅 Jan (date varies to coincide with camel breeding season)

ℹ Turkey Tourism www.tourismturkey.org

3 Sponge-diving

Isla Margarita, Venezuela

Hundreds of kilometres of Caribbean coastline provide Venezuela's prime diving spots with the palm-scattered Los Roques Archipelago National Park. Created in 1972, the 221 hectare (246 acre) park is located around 128 km (80 miles) from Caracas and contains one of the region's best-preserved barrier reefs. Shallow lagoons, thick mangrove forests and 350 islands and atolls lay in waters that offer exceptional visibility in January-February at up to 20 m (66 ft). To dive Los Roques is to experience a kaleidoscope of tropical fish and sponges with barracudas, snapper and grouper together with lurking stingrays on the sandy bottom.

Jan – Feb is quietest

Scuba Dive Margarita www.scubadivemargarita.com

Dive in gin-clear, pristine waters in Los Roques Archipelago National Park

4 Volcano Trekking

Maribios Volcanoes, Nicaragua

As Nicaragua's dry season begins, the lush vegetation of the Cordillera Los Maribios springs to life allowing climbers to trek this spiny volcanic ridge along emerald-green, bird-filled trails. This exhilarating full-on 60 km (38 mile) slog includes a string of over 21 volcanoes (some of which are still smoking). Trails traverse highland valleys, fumaroles and gnarled, twisted molten terrain of black sand, gravel and lava rock to 1,300 m (4,300 ft) over Lake Managua's leafy shores.

Year round, through routes are wettest Apr to Oct and at their clearest Dec and Jane

Nicaragua Tourist Office www.visitanicaragua.com

Tours Nicaragua www.toursnicaragua.com

5 Harbin Ice Festival

China

Dubbed 'Ice City', Harbin originated the Ice Festival in 1985 and offers visitors a dazzling array of illuminated ice-crafted lanterns. Snow-frosted sculptures depict scenes from traditional Chinese fairytales while fairy-lights twinkle around ice-carved lions, tigers and dragons – a striking winter spectacular in temperatures that can drop to –38°C (–36°F). Increasingly, modern technology plays a central role in many of Harbin's Ice Festival collections such as multi-coloured lasers and atmospheric neon-lit artificial mists. Festival activities follow an ice-and-snow theme from Alpine skiing and toboggan racing to swimming in the Songhua River's freezing depths.

📅 Starts on 5th Jan each year and lasts a month

❶ China National Tourist Office www.cnto.org
   Harbin website www.harbin.gov.cn

Marvel at China's wonder-packed, snow-frosted 'Ice City'

6 Fujairah Petroglyphs | ASIA

United Arab Emirates

Fujairah's January's temperatures plummet to a cool 22°C (72°F), making it the perfect month to explore the emirate's extraordinary ancient carved rocks. Believed to date back to the Iron Age, Fujairah's petroglyphs depict humped cattle from the salt deserts of Iran, Arabian camels and mythological serpents, while ancient script indicates a non-Islamic origin, possibly the tribal communities of the Oman Peninsula.

🗓 Pleasant spring-like Jan temperatures (around 21°C) are ideal for strenuous walking or hiking on this semi-arid terrain

ℹ www.fujairah-tourism.ae

7 Ethiopian Christmas | AFRICA

Ethiopia

Almost unique among African countries, Ethiopia was never colonized and so still follows the Julian calendar (as introduced to the world by Julius Caesar in 46BC). Unlike Western nations, Christmas (Lidet) falls on January 7th in Ethiopia. After an all-night church service that involves the congregation moving from one church to another, Ethiopia gets into the festive spirit with a game of *genna* – a hockey-style sport played with a curved stick and a round wooden ball by teams of young men. Derived from a game played by the shepherds (with crooks and rocks) while awaiting news of the saviour's birth, genna is now so popular that Christmas is increasingly known by the term Genna (also ganna and gena) – with festive games drawing crowds from miles around.

Arguably the most spiritual place to experience a traditional Genna is Lalibela, built by King Lalibela in the 12th century as Ethiopia's own Jerusalem. Pilgrims travel for many days to attend colourful Genna ceremonies in one of the 13 ancient churches carved from solid volcanic rock. On Christmas Eve, the whole night is spent outside praying, chanting and swaying side to side. Younger men dance around a drummer, leaping and jumping to achieve an almost trance-like state. Although the ceremony begins sedately it builds up to a frenzied crescendo with percussion-based music heard far and wide until the early hours.

On Christmas morning, a colourful procession forms led by three young men in robes brandishing whips. The cavalcade proceeds to a nearby hilltop cavern. Candles are issued to all that enter the church, the congregation walks around the rock-hewn chapel three times, before taking their place for the service – a three hour mass in which everyone stands. A Genna feast includes sourdough pancake (injera) served with doro wat (a spicy chicken stew) in decorated baskets. Gifts play a minor role, though children are sometimes given sweets or clothing. Ethiopia's traditional greeting is Melkam Genna! (meaning "Happy Christmas").

🗓 Jan 7th

ℹ Tourism Ethiopia www.tourismethiopia.org

8 Elvis's Birthday | NORTH AMERICA

Memphis, USA

Honouring Elvis on his birthday in Memphis has become a razzle-dazzle affair complete with rhinestone-clad impersonators, Elvis-themed music, movie clips, gospel tributes and basketball games. Fan Club diehards and devotees from across the globe gather at the front gates of Graceland at midnight to sing 'Happy Birthday' to

The King, setting celebrations in full swing. Expect Elvis-shaped cakes, Priscilla Presley, musicians from the Presley band, Elvis Bingo, Gala Dinners and Elvis parties.

🗓 Jan 8th (usually 3 days of birthday events)
ℹ Elvis Presley website www.elvis.com

9 Festival of the Desert | AFRICA

Essakane, Mali

Although less than a decade old, the Festival Au Desert in Essakane just two hours from Timbuktu boasts a loyal cult following. Originating from the region's Touareg festivities of ancient poetry, song and dance, the festival welcomes an eclectic bill of artists from Africa and all over the world. Over 30

musical genres celebrate global oral traditions in a largely non-commercialized event that also promotes world peace.

🗓 3 days, early Jan
ℹ Festival of the Desert www.festival-au-desert.org

10 National Voodoo Day | AFRICA

Ouidah Beach, Benin

Draped in animal skins with bones and fetish charms clattering, thousands of West Africans, Caribbean islanders and Western tourists descend on Benin for the annual Voodoo festival in the southern town of Ouidah. Voodoo rituals have been practiced by two-thirds of Benin's 6.7-million people since the end of the 16th century. Hundreds of spirit gods are honoured at clay

shrines with festivities that begin with the clatter of tambourines. Frenzied dances, incantations and deep trances last for several hours as over 10,000 participants in flowing robes rub shoulders with curious bystanders in a celebration of prayers, sacrifices and free-flowing libations.

🗓 Jan 10th
ℹ Republic of Benin Tourism www.benintourisme.com

11 Vintage Car Winter Marathon | EUROPE

Madonna di Campiglio, Italy

In mid-January each year, 420 km (260 miles) of icy roads in the ski resort town of Madonna di Campiglio play host to Italy's popular classic car Winter Marathon. An oddball assortment of antique cars fitted with spiked tyres and high-beam lights do battle with the elements on hair-raising bends, steep slopes and snow drifts. It's free to watch and relatively cheap to enter for those with nerves of steel.

23 3 days, mid-Jan

ℹ Winter Marathon www.wintermarathon.it

Madonna di Campiglio Tourism Board www.campiglio.to

Skid and slide along the snowy trails

Fresh snowfall adds to the treacherous conditions in Madonna de Campiglio

12 Diving Dragon's Breath Cave | AFRICA

Namibia

Namibia's intricate underground cave system offers some of the world's most exhilarating subterranean diving on a backdrop of semi-desert scenery, big game and river canyons. Namibia's 120 registered caves remain almost wholly undisturbed by man. Situated in the Otavi Mountain terrain of north-eastern Namibia is Dragon's Breath (Drachenhauchloch) cave – the world's largest underground lake. This vast body of water is an outer-worldly natural phenomenon, lying 60 m (197 ft) below ground in an enormous gnarled rock tavern.

Crystal clear sparkling waters boast a surface area of almost two hectares but are almost completely tourist-free given that they are only accessible using ropes and caving tools. Named for the hot air it exhales, Dragon's Breath Cave is thick with bat guano and a pungent smell that can be overpowering. With no sunlight, all lifeforms in the cave system rely on bat droppings as an energy source. At least 16 invertebrate species and one bat species inhabit the rocky depths ensuring the Lake Chamber is rich in organic deposits together with flotsam patches.

Locating the oh-so elusive entry hole in the ground for Dragon's Breath Cave requires exacting local knowledge. Yet once found this hidden crevice provides a glimpse into a jaw-dropping subterranean world. Before scuba diving in it, the fissure requires a combination of scrambling, spelunking and rappelling. As loose stones splash into the eerily dark waters below, cavers squeeze their way along a small shaft amidst rocky rubble. After an arduous near-vertical descent an unforgettable 100 m (330 ft) drop leads to water of extraordinary clarity that until the 1980s had lain undisturbed for thousands of years. This is for the adventurous and anyone with claustrophobic tendencies should definitely give the cave a miss.

📅 Year-round but avoid the soaring highs of summer

ⓘ Further information www.underwatervideo.co.za

The world's largest underground lake 60 m (197 ft) under gnarled rocks

13 Trekking in the Ankarana Reserve | AFRICA

Madagascar

While the Ankarana Reserve is generally inaccessible from February to April, mid-January is a great time to visit as the park is generally tourist free. A Jurassic-era limestone overlying a basaltic plain, the Ankarana massif is one of Madagascar's most rewarding hiking territories, boasting a mystical lost-world feel. Needle-thin pinnacles and rutted ridges sit in dense tropical tufts amidst deep canyons and gushing rivers. Remoteness ensures the reserve remains unaffected by deforestation. Rich in indigenous wildlife, it is home to wide-eyed lemurs, giant millipedes and mammoth land snails together with leaf-tailed lizards, Nile crocodiles and at least a dozen species of bat.

23 May - Jan, the dry season

❶ Wild Madagascar www.wildmadagascar.org

14 Sankranthi | ASIA

India

Sankranthi signifies the onset of harvest and is an important festival within India's many farming communities. Denoting the transition of the sun into Capricorn on its celestial path, Sankranthi is an auspicious celebration that takes many forms throughout India, depending on the community's focus. However, every celebration honours, worships and pays respect to Saraswati Maa (Goddess of Knowledge) during a period of reflection in which aspirants assess their goals in life. Pre-harvest ritual Bhogi is the time when people de-clutter their homes. Unwanted items are discarded and accumulated junk is burned. When Sankranthi arrives, departed ancestors are remembered with candies distributed to friends and family – and everyone wears new clothes to pray to their favourite God.

A harvest-time Indian ritual involving flames, reflection and prayers

23 14th Jan

❶ India Tourism www.incredibleindia.org

15 Turtle Nesting

Las Baulas, Costa Rica

During January and February, Costa Rica's Pacific Coastline prepares itself for the arrival of nesting Leatherback and Olive Ridley sea turtles. Traceable back to the Jurassic era over 150 million years ago, four of the seven surviving turtle species are found in Costa Rica. Females drag themselves ashore to lay their eggs in the sand at night in the exact region of their birth – impressive considering their foraging habitats could easily be 1,000 km (621 miles) away. These mass nesting episodes are locally referred to as arribadas, or arrivals. Locals will tell you that the arribadas begin three or four nights after the full moon. After laying, the turtles leave – and never return, abandoning their offspring to hatch unaided. Six to 13 weeks later, the hatchlings emerge and instinctively move to the water, beginning an arduous journey fraught with danger as tasty, defenceless snacks of the sea. Numerous participation projects for volunteers run from October to the end of February at the Las Baulas Marine National Park where turtles reach an average of 350 kg (772 lbs) and measure more than 1.5 m (about 5 ft) in length. Most programmes involve the conservation of offshore areas. Others require 'hands on' work involving close contact with adults and hatchlings, from the collection of data and the relocation of nests to promoting the plight of these magnificent creatures in a bid to stem declining survival rates.

📅 Jan – Feb (nesting season)

ℹ Costa Rica Tourism www.visitcostarica.com

Hatchlings embark on an arduous journey at Las Baulas National Marine Park

16 The Wildest of the Ati Atihan Festivals | ASIA

Kalibo, The Philippines

Meaning "make-believe", the Ati Atihan festival is named after the indigenous Ati peoples, held on the third week of January on the second Sunday after Epiphany. Famous for its wild frivolity, Ati Atihan is characterized by week-long frenzied merriments in honour of the Santo Niño. After a mass and rosary procession, dancers clad in multi-coloured masks and headdresses create an atmosphere evocative of Rio de Janeiro's hedonistic carnival (hence the nickname 'the Filipino Mardis Gras'). Syncopated crowds, bodies stained with black ash, pound the ground to mesmerising boom-boom-boom drum-beats. Kalibo on the island of Panay in the Aklan province is synonymous with the most decadent revelries. An important focus of Ati Atihan festivities is the tale of harvest thanksgiving and lasting friendship between the native Ati and early Spanish settlers. Ecstatic camaraderie unites the community during a festival of celebration for answered prayers and the silent whispers to God for food, happiness and good health. Impromptu parties depict these themes, bringing people out of their homes in the early afternoon to beat a drum, shake a rattle and join in wild dancing. Young and old throw themselves into the intoxicating melee, from shrieking children and troupes of swaying teens to septuagenarians in a swirl. Costumed processions represent every Aklan ethnicity in outfits made from abaca fibres, shells, feathers, plant leaves, sugar cane flowers, beads, and pieces of glass, metal and plastic. Colourful tribal displays, civic marches and sizzling food stalls piled high with palm wine provide a prelude to a final breathtaking procession in which different images of the Santo Niño are carried in a flame-lit cavalcade of bamboo torches – to cries of "Viva kay Santo Niño!"

An ecstatic post-Epiphany celebration in honour of Santo Niño

📅 Third week of Jan on the second Sunday after Epiphany
ℹ️ Philippines Tourism www.tourism.gov.ph

17 Alpine Polo

EUROPE

Klosters, Switzerland

Ice polo is played with considerable panache at mid-January's Berenberg Snow Polo tournament in the stylish Swiss Alpine resort of Klosters. Despite plummeting temperatures outside, crystal flutes of sparkling wine are served to a VIP-studded crowd in luxury heated tents. As night falls, polo teams from six nations battle it out in a nail-biting series of aggressive heats. Spectators are granted free admission to a public bar and lounge with views of fast-spinning chukka action while sizzling barbecues fire up grilled meats and sausages smothered in cheese. A highlight of Switzerland's winter calendar, the Berenbuerg tournament is the world's first night polo event on snow. Teams with a handicap of 8-9 compete on an oval field measuring 50 by 125 m (164 by 410 ft) with three players per team for the coveted Alpine Trophy. Artificial 'moonlighting' adds a subtle night-time glow with keen horsemanship and the finest polo ponies not only pitted against each other but also the unpredictability of ice and snow.

📅 Jan
ℹ Klosters Polo www.klosterspolo.com

18 Wilderness Woman Competition

NORTH AMERICA

Alaska, USA

It may make Women Libbers squirm, but the Talkeetna Bachelor Society contest for potential mates certainly separates the women from the girls. Events at the Wilderness Woman Contest vary each year, but offer plenty to smile about in the chill of a snowy Alaskan winter. With its tongue firmly in its cheek, the contest is only open to single women over 21. Entrants are judged on their firewood-hauling, water-fetching, snow-machining, fish-catching, moose-dispatching, ptarmigan-shooting, sandwich-making and beer-fetching: all desirable skills in a woman on the Last Frontier.

📅 Dec – Jan
ℹ Bachelors of Talkeentna www.bachelorsoftalkeetna.org
Alaska Wilderness Woman Competition
www.talkeetnachamber.org

19 Rajasthan Desert Festival

ASIA

Jaisalmer, India

Rajasthan's three-day Desert Festival brings a jamboree-like energy to Jaisalmer each January – February. Villagers from near and far celebrate the region's culture as acrobats, puppeteers and snake charmers and brightly-painted stalls are juxtaposed with folk dancers in swirling skirts near tents full of handcrafted goods. Contests include camel races, turban-tying and a Mr Desert competition against a backdrop of the Sam Sand dunes.

📅 3 days, Jan – Feb
ℹ India Tourism www.incredibleindia.org

20 Monte Carlo Rally
EUROPE

Monaco

As the longest-running event in world rally sport, the four-day Rallye Automobile Monte Carlo traces its roots to 1911. These days very little of the event is based in Monte Carlo, with most of the rally based hundreds of kilometres away in Valence. Perilous asphalt mountain paths are made even more treacherous by a tricky mix of weather and loose rocks. Stages are also run in darkness where cold temperatures ensure skiddy icy patches and freezing fog.

- 3 days, mid Jan
- Automobile Club of Monte Carlo www.acm.mc
  Monte Carlo Tourist Office www.visitmonaco.com

21 Dubai Food Festival
ASIA

United Arab Emirates

Fanatic foodies flock to numerous stalls, markets and restaurants at the week-long Dubai Food Festival in January - February each year. Alongside umpteen opportunities to sample local Arabic recipes, speciality dishes and cooking competitions are world-record-beating culinary feats. Past attempts include a bid to whip up the largest Manakish (baked dough topped with cheese or thyme or ground meat) on the planet using 10 kilos (22 lb) of thyme topping and more than 12 litres (3 gallons) of oil.

- Jan – Feb, week long festival
- Dubai Tourism www.dubaitourism.ae

22 Thaipusam
ASIA

Batu Caves, Kuala Lumpur, Malaysia

On the full moon in the Tamil month of Thai (Jan/Feb), Malaysia plays host to Thaipusam – an important Hindu festival celebrated with gusto in the Batu Caves north of Kuala Lumpur. Devotees prepare for the celebration by cleansing themselves through prayer and fasting before shaving their heads. They then undertake a pilgrimage during which they demonstrate their devotion with flesh piercing, fire walking and flagellation. Pilgrims claim they enter a trance and feel no pain. Thaipusam draws over 1-million Hindu devotees and tens of thousands of tourists. Processions depart from Sri Mahamariamman Temple along a 15 km (9 mile) route – an eight hour trek that culminates in a gruelling 272-step climb to the caves.

- On the full moon in the Tamil month of Thai (Jan/Feb)
- Tourism Malaysia www.tourismmalaysia.gov.my

23 Camping in Muscat | ASIA

Oman

With average temperatures around 22°C (72°F), January in Oman is fresh and spring-like and the perfect time to explore the dramatic, jagged ridges along the northern coastline. Rising above the Gulf's blue waters to around 3,000 m (9,843 ft), the Hajar Mountains boast rugged rocky trails used by generations of hunters, merchants and shepherds. Explore date groves and ancient mountain villages, camp on the high Sharaf al Alamayn plateau and enjoy far-reaching views across peaks and canyons or trek to the eastern spine to a gorgeous palm-strewn sandy beach.

23 Jan is spring-like, perfect for camping and trekking

❶ Oman Ministry of Tourism www.omantourism.gov.om

24 Spot Pink Freshwater Dolphins | SOUTH AMERICA

Puerto Narino, Colombia

Amazon's pretty coral-pink river dolphins (boto) can easily be seen on a journey along the Rio Yavari to magical Lago Tarapoto's shimmering expanse, 9 km (6 miles) west of Puerto Narino. Edged by Ficus trees and dotted with vast *Victoria amazonica* (giant lily), the shallows of Lago Tarapoto provide a fertile breeding ground for the Amazon's fish species. In January, the swollen rivers of the Amazon gush with heightened energy as tidal waters rise and fall in seasonal rhythm. Towering ferns, palms and tangled vines tumble into gurgling tides rich in nourishing plant sediments that are home to the largest collection of living non-human species on Earth.

23 Year-round

❶ OMACHA Foundation (Amazon Boto Dolphins) www.omacha.org

Friendly botos often sighted in the Amazon's fertile waters

25 Burns Night at a Highland Hotel | EUROPE

Scotland

Burns Suppers have been part of Scottish culture for about 200 years as a means of commemorating its best-loved bard, Robert Burns. Held annually on the evening of January 25th, one of the central features of the supper are the speeches and ceremonial rituals involving haggis. Burns immortalized this traditional Scottish dish in verse – and is honoured by it as a tribute to his memory. At Burns Suppers across Scotland, a Master of Ceremonies invites all present to receive the haggis – and it is duly carried in on a ceremonial platter accompanied by a lone piper in full national dress.

A short speech outlining the greatness of the poet is followed by a series of witty, addresses that include a toast to the 'lasses' in Burns' life. This prompts a humorous toast in response on behalf of the female guests, followed by more songs, poems and tributes. At the end of the feast, guests stand to link hands before singing Auld Lang Syne.

📅 Jan 25th

ℹ Robert Burns Archive www.robertburns.org
Scotland Tourist Board
www.scotland.org/burns-night/interactive

26 Cockroach Racing Championships | AUSTRALIA/PACIFIC

Queensland, Australia

In a break with tradition, Queenslanders forgo flag-raising and street parades on Australia Day to head to the pub for some serious cockroach racing – and lots of beer. In 1982, two barflies argued about the speed of roaches in Brisbane, each claiming the critters from their own neighbourhoods were the fastest. To test their alcohol-fuelled convictions, a race was staged for the bar crowd – and the rest is history. Today, the World Cockroach Championships at the Story Bridge Hotel, Kangaroo Point not only attracts sponsorship, TV coverage and live bands but is also described as "the greatest gathering of thoroughbred cockroaches in the known universe". Fancy dress is encouraged on a cockroach theme. Rules forbid all performance-enhancing substances, such as coffee, sugar and red cordial. Cheats are fined, or worse, publically declared as "not very Australian at all". Anticipation builds as the cockroaches arrive, carried in a clear-plastic lunchbox to a rousing bagpipe band. Top grade racers are announced by name over the loud speaker though inebriated fans can never really remember who is who. For most roaches, it's a rare trip out from under the fridge so nerves are commonplace – many refuse to budge, despite spraying beer and the screams of the crowd. Others make a mad dash to the edge of a 4 m (13 ft) ring where a megaphone-wielding judge calls out the winning name. In steeplechase events, a circular fence is used to "enhance the spectacle and test the roach talent". Entries are accepted on the day with roaches sold at the hotel door.

📅 Jan 26th (Australia Day)

ℹ Story Bridge Hotel www.storybridgehotel.com.au

27 Lerwick Up-Helly-Aa

Shetland, Scotland

Each year, on the last Tuesday in January, the Shetland Isles plays host to the Lerwick Up-Helly-Aa festival: a unique torch-lit celebration of a Viking past. The origins of the festival are the subject of conjecture: some say it harks back to the ancient Nordic practice of burning a galley as a sacrifice to the sun; others maintain it signifies the arrival of spring. Proceedings begin in the early evening when 'guizers' assemble in the town centre to form a parade led by the 'jarl', a fearsome looking warrior in full Viking dress. A thousand-strong procession of Viking costumed figures hold burning torches aloft. The festival reaches its peak at a specially constructed wooden Norse longboat when a signaling firework provides the cue to set the ship ablaze. After watching it burn, the crowds disperse as children sing Up-Helly-Aa songs while revelers dance until dawn.

🗓 Last Tuesday in Jan
❶ Lerwick Up-Helly-Aa www.uphellyaa.org
   Shetland Tourist Bureau www.visitshetland.com

A torch-lit parade and festival from Nordic times

28 Hay Festival

Cartagena, Colombia

Cartagena's Hay Festival has become Latin America's essential detour for sun-seeking literati. Not only has it captured the hearts and minds of locals but it has also attracted a high-pedigree of Latin American literary talent and some high-profile international artists. Cartagena is also the adopted home of 'Gabo', Gabriel Garcia Marquez, author of *A Thousand Years of Solitude* and Colombia's Nobel laureate. During the Hay Festival it offers free

poetry readings, recitals and performances in plazas, churches, gardens and parks. Cartagena's 16th-century colonial architecture in bold, bubblegum hues provides a stunning backdrop to torch-lit plays and dramatic adaptations.

🗓 4-day festival, end of Jan - early Feb
❶ Hay Festival Cartagena www.hayfestival.com/Cartagena
   Travel the Unknown www.traveltheunknown.com

29 Ski the Rockies
| NORTH AMERICA

Banff, Canada

In late November the first snow begins to fall on the Canadian Rockies marking the start of a six-month season that boasts what locals claim is the best powder snow in the world. Banff National Park, a World Heritage Site bristling with rugged alpine beauty and abundant wildlife, forms the heart of skiing in the Canadian Rockies. Over 240 trails and more than 3,116 hectares (7,700 acres) of pristine snow can be found in three outstanding ski resorts – Norquay, Sunshine Village and Lake Louise.

📅 Late Jan (after a good dump of snow)
ℹ Canadian Tourism www.canada.travel

30 St Benedict's Caverns
| AUSTRALIA/PACIFIC

Waikato, New Zealand

Dubbed "the prettiest cave in New Zealand", St Benedict's Cavern sits beneath acres of lush, rolling farmland in a private field. Through a Hobbit-style hatched door discover a 40 x 100 m (131 x 328 ft) troglodyte chamber adorned with curious crevices and plunging fissures reached by a couple of abseils and a spectacular underground flying fox. In near-dry cosy warmth, explore a mysterious subterranean terrain under vast twisted stalactites and limestone crystals, ancient fossils and mammoth rocks.

📅 Late Jan
ℹ Canadian Tourism www.canada.travel

31 The Desert Coast
| SOUTH AMERICA

Peru

Peru's Pacific coast is as diverse as it is spectacular. Leave Lima's congested traffic behind to venture into an aged landscape of Nazca geoglyphs and outer-worldly desert set between the Pacific Ocean and the Andes Mountains. Fertile valleys of cotton and sugarcane stretch to grass-fringed beaches and quaint fishing ports. Fossil-rich archaeological ruins hug the tourist trail while condors, sea turtles, dolphins and hundreds of pink flamingos hide amidst the coastal scenery of the Paracas National Reserve, dubbed 'the baby Galapagos'.

📅 Dec - Mar
ℹ Peru Tourism www.peru.info

Full Moon Party, Koh Phangan, Thailand

February

1 Samba Schools at the Rio Carnival | SOUTH AMERICA

Rio de Janeiro, Brazil

Thousands of volunteers help to oil the wheels of the Rio Carnival, one of the wildest parties on earth. To ensure the dancing kings and queens of the Samba Schools can sway their way through the streets, teams of helpers prepare the procession. Got a flair for textiles and costumes? Then join the Samba School workshops for a full cultural immersion, from pressing glitzy costumes and painting multi-coloured floats to ensuring Rio's procession is at its vibrant best.

📅 4 days, 40 days before Easter
ℹ Responsible Travel www.responsibletravel.com
    Rio de Janeiro Samba Schools www.rio-carnival.net

Flamboyant, sassy, ritzy and glitzy at the largest Carnival on Earth

2 Nicaraguan Poetry Festival | SOUTH AMERICA

Granada, Nicaragua

Granada's vibrant early-February poetry festival is Nicaragua's national celebration of verse and the largest such event in Central America. Declared a Cultural and Natural Patrimony of Humanity by UNESCO, Granada's colonial architectural splendour draws artists from all over the country together with a high-calibre pool of international talent. Granada's wide, cobblestone streets, paved plazas, handsome churches and markets provide an inspiring setting for poets, local residents and tourists alike. Each year's festival honours a famous Nicaraguan poet, such as José Coronel Urtecho,

leader of the Vanguardia literary movement between 1927 and 1929, and is run in conjunction with "Aquí está Granada" (meaning "Here is Granada") – a celebration of the Nicaraguan capital. Expect free poetry recitals, traditional cultural ceremonies, open-air concerts, literary discussions and folkloric dancing.

📅 6-day festival, mid-Feb
ℹ Nicaragua Poetry Festival
    www.festivalpoesianicaragua.org.ni

3 Pag Winter Festival | EUROPE

Croatia

Dressing up is essential to the storyline at Pag's annual Winter Carnival where the principal act involves a man clad in women's clothes. One of Croatia's northern Dalmatian islands, Pag is third largest in the Kvarner Gulf. Crowds form in front of the parish priest's house or in the main square on carnival night – only then can the performance begin.

Expect a high-drama plot involving two young boys, a salesman, a musician and Turkish rulers – together with a lead female slave named Robinja.

🗓 Feb
ℹ Croatian Tourist Board www.croatia.hr

4 Crocodiles on Adelaide River | AUSTRALIA/PACIFIC

Northern Territories, Australia

During the Northern Territory's wet season from November to March rivers burst across the flood plains and roads remain underwater for months. Saltwater crocs, the most dangerous reptile in Northern Australia, head upriver to breed, spreading out over a wide area. Crocodiles can be seen up-close during wetland tours of the flooded plains.

Kingfishers and corellas gather in flocks beside the Adelaide River while wild pigs and buffalo forage in the waterlogged grasses.

🗓 Year-round (but the wet season adds some excitement!)
ℹ Adelaide River Cruises www.adelaiderivercruises.com.au

5 Sapporo Snow Festival | ASIA

Hundreds of snow sculptures are illuminated by lasers and lights

Sapporo, Japan

Sapporo's annual week-long Snow Festival is a dazzling ice-frosted spectacle that lures over two million visitors onto the streets. Odori Park, International Square and Susukino boast 300 laser-lit snow sculptures with elaborate displays of Sapporo's winter delicacies, such as crab, cuttlefish and salmon, frozen inside the ice. Attractions include a 100 m (328 ft) slide, snow-carved maze, hot-air balloon flights and snow rafting.

🗓 1 week, early Feb
ℹ Sapporo Snow Festival www.snowfes.com
Japan National Tourist Authority www.jnto.go.jp

6 Celebrate Bob Marley's Birthday | NORTH AMERICA

Jamaica commemorates the irrepressible rhythmic pulse of the 'Godfather of Reggae'

Kingston, Jamaica

Bob Marley's image and music is everywhere in Jamaica, despite it being almost three decades since the reggae legend's death in 1981, at 36. On 6th February concerts, recitals and festivals honour his birth in 1945. Marley helped to propel reggae to worldwide popularity with his smoky tenor voice and loping beat. In 1964, he formed The Wailers with Peter Tosh and Bunny Livingston, recording hit after hit. He mixed his rhythmic pulses with a strong political message, reinforcing nonviolence. He also endorsed the Rastafarian religion to become reggae's seminal figure and foremost practitioner and emissary.

Jamaica is the Caribbean's third-largest island and also one of the most colourful with powdery white sand beaches and vibrant tropical blooms on a backdrop of hazy-blue mountain peaks. In vibrant Kingston, the Bob Marley Museum, once the Tuff Gong studio, established by Marley in 1965, commemorates Jamaica's musical heritage. On Marley's birthday hundreds of reggae pilgrims from all across the world descend on the museum or make the trek to the small village of Nine Miles several hours outside of Kingston – the reggae star's final resting place. Some simply pop open a can of Jamaica's favourite beer as a tribute. Others crank up Marley's debut release track, "Judge Not". Or simply find a reggae-drenched local bar in which to celebrate the root of Marley's music – the island and the red, yellow, green Jah-love Rastafarian culture itself.

📅 Feb 6th
ℹ Tel: 876 927 9 152 www.bobmarley-foundation.com

7 Chinese New Year | ASIA

Pingyao, China

Founded in the 14th century, Pingyao is famous for its exceptionally well-preserved Han architecture. Encircled by a 6 km (4 mile) city wall and a 3 m (10 ft) moat, Pingyao's pretty lantern-slung alleyways, handsome courtyards and black-and-grey houses are accessed via an imposing drawbridge. Join the New Year celebrations at this unique UNESCO World Heritage site where the 1990s film *Raise the Red Lantern* was shot.

⊞ Jan 20th – Feb 20th, according to the Lunar Calendar
❶ China National Tourist Office www.cnto.org

Enjoy the revelry amidst Pingyao's pretty lantern-strewn streets

8 Toronto WinterCity Festival | NORTH AMERICA

Toronto, Canada

Toronto's 14-day celebration of culture, creativity and cuisine attempts to heat up the city in winter with a sizzling trio of festivals rolled into one. Free concerts by Canadian bands wow the crowds while storytellers narrate contemporary classics and modern dance troupes dazzle audiences after dark. Sculptors craft vast works from metal, clay and fire to the music of budding DJs. Over 130 restaurants offer diners a chance to experience some of Toronto's finest dishes amidst street stalls and firework displays.

⊞ 2 weeks, late Jan – mid Feb
❶ Toronto Tourism www.toronto.ca

9 Horse Racing | EUROPE

St Moritz, France

For over 120 years, oh-so glamorous St Moritz has hosted the spectacular White Turf horse race. High society, top jockeys and some of the world's most successful race horse owners converge at this showcase of pure-bred horses on a backdrop of snow-capped mountains. Galloping horses carry daring riders in this fast-paced skikjöring event - a social highlight of the winter season that attracts 25,000 spectators from across the globe.

⊞ Weekends through Feb
❶ White Track Events www.whitetracks.co.uk

10 Yukon Quest Husky Race

Alaska, USA

The 1,600 km (994 mile) Yukon Quest may lack the global publicity of the Iditarod (the 'other' premier long distance dog sled racing event) – but is arguably the tougher of the two. Spread over four summits over 900 m (3,000 ft), the Quest trail is an epic challenge in the heart of the Arctic winter through some of the most pristine wilderness remaining in North America. Checkpoints are as far as 320 km (200 miles) apart over some of the most treacherous terrain on the planet. Temperatures can drop to -40°C (-40°F) and blizzards and white-outs are common. The Quest is almost as gruelling for spectators with snatched sleep in the back of a truck and a diet of hastily-eaten moose stew.

Unlike the Iditarod, a musher must demonstrate his ability to compete long distances ahead of entering the Yukon Quest by completing at least one 480 km (300 mile) race and an additional 300 km (200 mile) plus race, for a minimum of 800 km (500 miles) within the 42 months prior to the race's start. The race is well-respected, attracting tough, talented individuals

One of the toughest sledding challenges on Earth across perilous ice-clad summits in temperatures of -40°C (-40°F)

full of daring do. While the purse is moderate, this doesn't deter the world's big name mushers from entering. Most view the Quest's low-key media presence and isolation as a positive plus. Dogs and their drivers were essential in opening up the backcountry in the 1898 Gold Rush that brought a rush of individuals to the north. Sledding became a vital mode of transport, not only to the Klondikers, but to trappers and traders as well; the mighty Yukon River was their major winter highway. In 1983, a small group of mushers in Fairbanks conjured up a new dog sled race along the old mail, trade, and trapping routes. In 1984 the first Yukon Quest was run. Tagged 'the toughest dogsledding race in the world', the event has remained wholly faithful to the spirit and history of the north. Competitors are alone with their dogs for hundreds of miles – and, except at the race's halfway point at Dawson City, they're allowed no outside help.

📅 2 weeks, Feb

ℹ Yukon Quest www.yukonquest.com

11 Hadaka Matsuri (Naked Man Festival) | ASIA

Okayama City, Japan

Each year a large number of brave souls in skimpy loincloths take part in the Naked Man Festival (Hadaka Matsuri) in Okayama, Japan in on a wintry night. Celebrated for over 1,200 years, the festival centres on a running Naked Man (the shin-otoko) who becomes a chosen vessel for all the bad luck of his fellows. They can rid themselves of evil spirits should they be fast enough to touch his skin en route to a shrine. At the temple, the Naked Man undergoes a lengthy purification ritual that once marked the culmination of the 14-day New Year festivities in ancient Japan. Originally, community elders were presented with paper talisman by the monks but, over time, the amulets were replaced by sticks and in its modern incarnation, the festival builds into a testosterone frenzy when the sticks are released into the crowd as midnight strikes.

📅 Mid – Feb

ℹ Japanese National Tourist Authority www.jnto.jp

A 1,200-year-old testosterone frenzy

12 Full Moon Party | ASIA

Koh Phangan, Thailand

Every month, Koh Phangan's gently swaying palm trees and alabaster-sand beaches erupt into into festival of global notoriety. Hailed as the world's biggest beach bash, the Full Moon Party attracts barefoot hedonists from across the globe. More than a dozen sound systems run the length of Had Rin beach as every beach bar DJ cranks up the volume – and up to 30,000 raging lunar party animals max-up the party vibe.

📅 Year-round (according to the moon)

ℹ Thailand Tourism www.tourismthailand.org

13 Volcan del Totumo

Colombia

From a distance, the Volcán de Lodo El Totumo looks like a giant anthill: a conical mound rising up from the ground around 50 km (31 miles) northeast of Cartagena on Colombia's steamy Caribbean coast. Legend has it that the Volcán once spouted fire, but a local priest, seeing the 15 m (50 ft) hillock as the work of the devil, sprinkled it with holy water. The flames slowly extinguished, drowning the devil in mud. Today, the mud-filled crater attracts people from near and far keen to take a therapeutic dip in its warm, cappuccino-thick depths. Yield to this nutrient-rich natural bath and all manner of ailments are cured and fatigued limbs soothed. A makeshift wooden banister leads the way to the top of the volcano where visitors can bathe from dawn 'til dusk for a small fee.

Mud-dipping at the Volcán is a fun-filled ritual for families and friends that involves lying back in a brown, sludgy gloop full of natural minerals and nutrients great for the complexion and giggling a lot. While in this hippo-like state, don't be surprised if a gaggle of local villagers turn up – a massage is often part of the deal. A neighbouring lagoon provides the perfect place for a post-dip clean-up – you'll find buckets by the fence and recycled plastic bottles should you want some mud to take away.

📅 Year-round, through routes are at their clearest in Dec – Feb
ℹ️ Nicaragua Tourist Office www.visitanicaragua.com
  Tours Nicaragua www.toursnicaragua.com

14 St Valentine's Feast

Terni, Italy

Dubbed the House of Love, Terni's cathedral is the final resting place of the Saint of Love himself. Little is known about this enigmatic figure. He is believed to have been born in AD175 and martyred almost 100 years later in 273 – though why is subject to great debate. However, San Valentino defied the emperor Aurelian in a tale of the triumph of love over cultural differences, allowing Sabino, a pagan Roman soldier and local Christian girl Serapia to wed. Today

couples descend on Terni on February 14 each year to take or renew their marriage vows. The annual San Valentino Feast is a month of celebrations themed around love and romance, from candlelit masses to art exhibitions, poetry recitals and firework displays.

📅 Feb 14th
ℹ️ San Valentino Terni www.sanvalentinoterni.com
  Town of Terni www.comune.terni.it

15 Flamenco in the Old Quarter

Madrid, Spain

Madrid's flamenco scene is firmly entrenched in the city's cobblestone old quarter where daylight hours are a relaxed affair of pigeon-scattered plazas, pavement cafés and snoozing street-corner traders. After dark, the city bursts into life as restaurants and bars fill and music flows as freely as the wine. Madrileños joke that the day begins at 10pm when the lights dim, clubs open and crowds swell into the city – an exaggeration, but almost true. The city's side-street tablaos (establishments with a stage used for flamenco performances) throw open their doors to an eager audience keen to ignite the shadows with the fiery passion of dance. Stunning interiors adorned with traditional tilework, boldly painted ceramic murals, scrubbed wooden floors and lime-washed walls evoke the aura of another age.

Gypsy-originated flamenco rejects formality preferring improvised movements that mirror the mood of the moment with great exuberance and intensity. Young and old radiate to such venues as Corral de la Morería, Café de Chinitas, Torres Bermejas and Taberna Casa Patas where flamenco's finest performers include Chaquetón, Remedios Amaya, Chano Lobato and La Niña Pastori – to name but a few. A month-long Festival Flamenco Caja Madrid at the Albéniz Theater showcases the best in flamenco. A dance genre characterized by rapid passages and audible footwork, flamenco is thought to derive from the Arabic music traditions of Moorish times. Strumming guitars follow the rhythms as dancers take to the floor, chins perfectly poised and arms aloft. In Madrid, flamenco is the dance of the people with visitor participation welcome to encouraging stamps and shouts. Simply allow your

A fiery, passion-filled click of heel on tile

body to feel the rhythm (the *compás*) rather than mechanically count the beats. Close your eyes and yield to the escalating syncopated tempo of raw emotion, lust, joy, passion and mournful lament.

📅 Year-round (but avoid the touristy summer season)

ℹ Madrid Tourism www.turismomadrid.es

16 Oruro Carnival | SOUTH AMERICA

Bolivia

As the folklore capital of Bolivia, Oruro's carnival is the nation's largest cultural gathering and an important Ito festival for the Uru people with rituals that centre on the goddess of Pachamama (Mother Earth). The Virgen del Socavon (Virgin of the Mineshaft) is also honoured during the three day festival. Re-enactments of a Spanish-era conquest provide a fire-cracker-filled highlight together with dozens of indigenous groups, 30,000 dancers and 10,000 musicians who form a procession along a 4 km (2.5 mile) route.

📅 Mid-Feb - Mar (3 days)

ℹ️ Bolivia Tourism www.turismobolivia.bo

17 Carnaval de Barranquilla | SOUTH AMERICA

Colombia

The hedonistic Carnaval de Barranquilla is one of South America's most explosive festivals and the largest in Colombia. On Saturday, La Battala de Flores (Flower Battle) starts the celebrations in which symbolic bullets of war are replaced with the flowers of peace. Sunday sees thousands of costume-clad revellers join La Gran Parada (The Great Parade). The cavalcade features drum-beat dances and animal masks painted in black, red, white and yellow. On Monday, a 24-hour open-air concert of pumping Caribbean music dominates El Festival de Orquetas before the figurative burial of Joselito Carnaval on Tuesday. Joselito was, so the story goes, a hard-working Barranquilla coach driver who drank too much during Carnaval one year. On seeing his slumped body, the merry-makers assume he is dead. They realise their mistake when they hear him snore, so decide to conduct a mock funeral cortege as a joke. Today crowds of 'mourners' cry over the death of the coachman. The re-enactment signifies the end of the carnival – when Barranquilla can finally get some sleep.

Music-filled processions and dancing parades

📅 4 days, Feb - Mar

ℹ️ Barranquilla Carnival www.carnavaldebarranquilla.org

18 Mumbai Film Festival | ASIA

India

India's colossal film industry dwarfs Hollywood's output by 2:1 with over a thousand movie releases per year. Films are a national obsession – well over 14-million Indians visit the country's thousands of cinemas each day. As the epicentre of India's film industry, Mumbai is home to umpteen performing arts colleges, casting agencies, producers, directors, film crews and scriptwriters – and a magnet for every star-struck hopeful keen to secure a role in the latest flick. February heralds the city's much-anticipated five-day annual Film Festival, a time when every new Indian release ramps up publicity, crowds of would-be actors tout their CV and a million extras fulfil their Bollywood dream.

🗓 7 days, mid – late Feb
ℹ Mumbai Film Festival www.mumbaifilmfest.com
India Tourist Board www.incredibleindia.org

19 Climb Jebel Toubkal | AFRICA

Morocco

A number of routes lead up North Africa's highest peak at 4,167 m (13,671 ft) in the Toubkal National Park, 63 km (39 miles) south of Marrakech. Imlil is the least technical route up to Jebel Toubkal – the so-called "Roof of North Africa' – and avoids the undignified scrambling required by most Atlas trails. Routes are impassable until the snow clears at blossom time in late February to April. Climbing up to this impressive massif takes two days along quiet trails with magnificent views. Be sure to pack a good map and hire a Tachelhit-speaking local guide.

🗓 Feb – Apr (blossom time)
ℹ Morocco Tourism www.visitmorocco.com

20 Fly-fishing in Patagonia | SOUTH AMERICA

Chile

Twisted glaciers, fjords, slow-shifting icebergs and jagged mountains characterise the awesome landscape around capital Coyhaique where clear lakes, rivers, Alpine streams and lagoons are rich in numerous species of fish. One of the finest places to fly-fish for trout, Patagonia boasts numerous secluded spots only accessible by boat. Temperate rainforests provide a home to hundreds of species of birds while otters, minks and foxes can often be sighted from the riverbank. Fish mid-November to early May, though February is a prime month for snagging brown trout of 2–3.5 kg (4-8 lbs).

🗓 Mid-Nov – early May with Feb the prime trout season
ℹ Chile Tourism Office www.visit-chile.org

21 Shrove Tuesday (Pancake Day) | EUROPE

Olney, Bedfordshire, England

People used to cook pancakes to use up the perishable store-cupboard items forbidden during Lent, including eggs, fat, milk and flour. Today, Shrove Tuesday is observed by the cooking and eating of pancakes 47 days before Easter Sunday. It is also celebrated by the traditional practice of Pancake Races throughout the UK – most notably in the 18th-century market town of Olney in Bedfordshire. Here, townsfolk gather to see one of the country's oldest Pancake Races believed to date back to 1445. Legend has it that one woman, engrossed in cooking pancakes, forgot the time until she heard the church bells calling everyone to the shriving service. She ran to the church, clad in her apron and with skillet in hand. In following years, other women of Olney got into the act. The one reaching the church steps first was kissed by the verger, or bell-ringer – a greeting that became known as the "Kiss of Peace". Today small teams of costumed competitors flip pancakes in a pan as they run through the town. Crowds cheer on their favourite teams and sizzling pancake stalls offer plenty of opportunity to sample the pre-Lenten staple, sprinkled with sugar and freshly squeezed lemon juice or served with a dollop of syrup.

📅 Feb – Mar (47 days before Easter Sunday)

ℹ Bedfordshire Tourism www.experiencebedfordshire.co.uk

One of the world's oldest pancake races dating back to the 15th century

22 Mardi Gras

NORTH AMERICA

New Orleans, USA

Mardi Gras has been celebrated in cities worldwide since 1699 but for many Americans, New Orleans *is* Mardis Gras – no one does it better. Culminating with oh-so hedonistic Fat Tuesday in February, this traditional season of carnival merriment heralds the penitential season of Lent with Cajun feasting, pumping jazz music, garish outfits and dance. Dozens of lively parades provide a colourful prelude to Mardi Gras day, so whether you are on St Charles Avenue with the family, catching glittery beads from a Central Business District balcony or enjoying the hand-sewn intricate costumes on Canal before a night of partying in the French Quarter, be prepared to scream "Throw me something, Mister!" really loud in order to fill a bag full of inexpensive trinkets tossed from each outlandish, multi-coloured passing float.

🗓 Feb - Mar

ℹ Mardi Gras New Orleans www.mardigrasneworleans.com
   New Orleans Tourism www.neworleansonline.com

23 Mashramani ('Mash')

SOUTH AMERICA

Guyana

Mashramani (or 'Mash' as it known by the locals) heralds a full-on celebration of multi-coloured costumed parades, steel band music and dance to commemorate the Birth of the Republic in 1966. Each of Guyana's indigenous tribal groups wears its ancestral dress in a showcase of the country's multiethnic make-up and religious mix (Guyana is roughly half Christian, a third Hindu, and a tenth Islamic). Calypso competitions with witty social commentaries are also an integral part of 'Mash', held each year on 23rd February.

🗓 Feb 23rd

ℹ Guyana Tourism www.guyana-tourism.com

24 Battle of the Oranges

EUROPE

Ivrea, Italy

The Ivrea Carnival commemorates an era of uprisings against bygone tyrannies when wars were said to have been won by throwing stones. Today, these fights for liberty use softer ammunition – oranges. Only excess fruits are used in this zesty re-enactment of old battles in which costumed legions of 10,000 troops pelt each other with oranges. Participants in the Battle of the Oranges wear red hats as a symbol of liberty – with hatless bystanders considered the 'enemy' and therefore a justifiable target for a spattering of juice or pith.

🗓 Feb 24th

ℹ www.italiantouristboard.co.uk

25 Buenos Aires Tango Festival | SOUTH AMERICA

Argentina

Since the earliest days of liquor-soaked brothels of the slums of Buenos Aires, tango has been emblematic of Argentina's intense, sensual dance. Mesmeric, moody and oh-so stylish, the tango effuses with eroticism and raw, steaming, sexual tension. During spring, many of Buenos Aires' several thousand tango bars and dancehalls stage free displays throughout the capital during the seven-day annual Tango Festival. Classes run from beginners to masters, led by world-class dancers, again all for free, together with orchestral concerts, film screenings and tango fashion parades.

📅 2 weeks, late Feb – early Mar
ℹ️ Festival de Tango www.festivaldetango.gov.ar

26 Venice Carnivale | EUROPE

Venice, Italy

Venice's masked festival can be traced back to the 14th century when nobility and commoners alike donned elaborate disguises. For Carnival season only Venice turned its social order temporarily on its head. Masks often depict Commedia dell'Arte characters. Others are more sinister and worn with long sweeping cloaks. The 18th century was an era of "anything goes" that saw gambling dens, brothels, theatres, cafés, liquor stores (licensed and illicit) and circus booths featuring exotic animals, tightrope walkers, fire-eaters and jugglers do a roaring trade. Today, the Carnival attracts crowds of costumed revellers of all ages and nationalities – each hell-bent on entering into the spirit of things. Festivities run up until the Tuesday before Ash Wednesday with all-night music and dancing, though these days Venice's ritzy balls are more genteel than debauched.

📅 14 days, Feb
ℹ️ Venice Carnival www.carnevale.venezia.it
Venice Tourism www.turismovenezia.it

Costumed revellers enjoy masked anonymity

27 Albatross Chick Hatching

Otago Peninsula, New Zealand

A soaring Albatross is an unforgettable spectacle. Held aloft on slim wings with a span of up to 3 m (10 ft), birds swoop at speeds of over 115 kph (71 mph). Breeding birds arrive at Taiaroa Head on New Zealand's Otago Peninsula each September, building nests early November before laying a single white egg weighing up to 0.5 kg (1 lb) in spring. Albatross pairs share incubation duty in spells of two to eight days over a period of 11 weeks. Tucked at the foot of Taiaro Head, the Royal Albatross Centre protects the colony from interference. Hatching takes place late January and February.

23 Hatching takes place late Jan - Feb

ⓘ Royal Albatross Centre www.albatross.org.nz

Otago Peninsula Tourism www.otago-peninsula.co.nz

A single egg is nurtured by breeding pairs

28 Slow Boat Down the Mekong

Laos

At 4,180 km, (2,600 miles) the mighty Mekong River is the 10th largest river on earth and the lifeblood of Laos. Bounded by the inaccessible icy wastes of the eastern Tibetan plateau and the South China Sea, it flows south to east through China, Myanmar, Thailand, Laos, Cambodia and Vietnam, emptying into the South China Sea through a wide delta south of Ho Chi Minh City. Today, cruises along this ancient cargo route require a steel-hulled vessel with the weather in February hot, sunny and dry – ideal for interacting with fishermen and villagers on the riverbanks as the watercourse winds its turbulent way through jungles, mountains, teak plantations, and farmland.

23 Nov – Mar

ⓘ Way to Mekong Tours www.waytomekong.com

29 Leap Year at Greenwich Royal Observatory | EUROPE

London, England

In the Gregorian calendar, a year is 365 days long – unless, that is, the year is exactly divisible by four. In that instance, an extra day is added to February to make the year 366 days long – unless it is the last year of a century, e.g. 1800, 1900, 2000. Then it is only a leap year if it is exactly divisible by 400 – 1900 wasn't but 2000 was. Why the need for this bizarre calculus? It's all do with bringing the calendar year in line with the length of the Earth's orbit around the Sun. A year is defined as being the interval between two successive passages of the Sun through the vernal equinox. By adding an extra day (or not), the seasons always occur during the same months.

Sound complicated? That's nothing compared to Greenwich Mean Time (GMT) – a single time zone setting and the baseline for the world invented by Sandford Fleming, an early pioneer of the global 24-hour clock. By 1855, around 98 per cent of the clocks in Britain were set to GMT although it was not made the law until 25 years later.

Today, the Royal Greenwich Observatory remains the iconic home of Greenwich Mean Time – a place where you can stand with a foot in both Western and Eastern hemispheres. At precisely 1300 hours every day since 1833, its red time-ball has fallen to enable ships to set their clocks accurately. Britain's first telegraph cable linked it to a similar time-ball in Walmer on the south-east coast for the benefit of shipping in the English Channel. Since 1884, the world has set its clocks according to the time of day on the Meridian of Greenwich, longitude 0° – an imaginary line joining the North and South Poles through the dead centre of a specialized telescope installed at the Observatory in 1851.

The Royal Observatory houses a unique collection of historic timepieces and navigational instruments in exhibits that tell the story of time and astronomy and the origins of the Observatory itself. Take a stroll around the rooms of the Astronomer Royal; enjoy shows in the Observatory's tiny Planetarium and visit one of the few camera obscuras in the courtyard, Monday to Sunday 10am-5pm.

📅 Feb 29th (Leap Year)

ⓘ Royal Observatory Greenwich www.nmm.ac.uk

The iconic home of GMT

March

St David's Day | EUROPE

Disneyland, Paris, France

To reflect the high number of British visitors to Disneyland Paris each year, some British cultural festivals have been added to its calendar, including St. David's Day. In typical Disney style the Welsh theme has been sprinkled with plenty of razzle-dazzle fairy dust with rousing male voice choirs belting out Land of My Fathers over the turrets of Cinderella's Castle. A stage showcases up-and-coming Welsh bands while the scrumptious aromas of laver bread (Cawl Lafwr), potato pie (Pastai Datws) and leek soup (Cawl Cennin) waft from a speciality food hall. Naturally Mickey and Minnie get in on the action dressed in the full national costume of Wales. Other familiar associations of Welshness abound from sheep and daffodils to Celtic symbols with a dramatic explosion of white, red, and green fireworks a stunning sunset finale.

🎟 3-day festival around Mar 1st
ⓘ Disneyland Paris www.disneylandparis.com

Gay Mardi Gras Parade | AUSTRALIA/PACIFIC

Sydney, Australia

It's hard to think of another major city that has embraced its gay pride event quite as Sydney has done. Sydney's Mardi Gras unites gay and straight communities and captures the imagination of party-lovers across the world. Born as a defiant statement of gay rights in 1978, the Mardi Gras is now Australia's biggest tourist attraction drawing thousands from overseas, including 10 jumbo jets from San Francisco alone. Providing a warm, sunny escape from the Northern Hemisphere winter, Sydney is one of the world's most diverse and tolerant cities. Many fly across the world again and again to enjoy this iconic event, generating an estimated $AUS 38 million ($US 27 million) for the regional economy.

Mardi Gras is three weeks packed full of culture, entertainment and social occasions that remains the one truly global gay annual event. Over 100 different arts events combine with a 70,000-person daytime picnic (Fair Day) and the Parade Post-Parade Party – before one of the famous parties in the world erupts in a risqué explosion of sequins, false eyelashes and feather boas. Sydney's Gay & Lesbian Mardi Gras Parade was named one of the world's top ten costume parades in the world by Condé Nast and thrusts the city into a state of feverish excitement. Around half-a-million spectators line the two-mile urban route to cheer on a flotilla of outrageously flamboyant decorated floats. Grotesque satirical effigies prompt boos and catcalls while elaborate costumes pay homage to gay icons. One of the largest parades in recent years featured 250 Kylie Minogue impersonators dubbed the 'Impossible Princesses'.

🎟 3 weeks Feb – Mar (Saturday parade)
ⓘ Sydney Mardi Gras www.mardigras.org.au

A defiant and dramatic gay rights parade since 1978

Night of the Witches | NORTH AMERICA

Catemaco, Mexico

Mexico's Noches de Brujas (Night of the Witches) is a spirited celebration of native pagan traditions. Catemaco, a small lakeside town close to Veracruz Close draws witch doctors from all over the world to a hubbub of alternative medicine, spiritual healing and magical curative potions. Rest assured – this is an ancient ritual cherished by the Mexican people for centuries, not a new-breed festival reserved for tourists, so expect cigar-smoking mystics, shaman and wild-haired practitioners of the supernatural.

📅 1st Friday in Mar
ℹ️ Mexico Tourist Board www.visitmexico.com

4 The Sacred Sonoran Desert | NORTH AMERICA

Arizona, USA

According to mystics, the Sonoran Desert boasts a highly concentrated spiritual might that is conducive to prayer, meditation and healing. Like a magnet, it draws people from all over the world. Steeped in spiritual legend, it remains a powerful force in Native American culture where the positive healing energy of the land is said to enrich mind, body and soul. Sedona sits at the foot of the Mogollon Rim, the southernmost part of the Colorado Plateau: a spiny ridge that extends for 322 km (200 miles) across central Arizona to the White Mountains at an average height of 2,134 m (7,000 ft). Originating from wind-blown sand, Sedona's captivating colours span a myriad of crimson hues, from blood-orange and brick-red to magenta-pink – all around 250-million years old. Dozens of ancient trails lead to canyons and towering pinnacles that are rich in tales of Palatkwapi shaman and gifted Hopi healers. Spring brings conferences, workshops and healing centres led by the Sedona Metaphysical Spiritual Association. Achieve heightened spiritual awareness to re-connect amongst healing turquoise crystals and tribal burial sites. Realign chakras and balance energies whilst discovering the ancient health rituals of the indigenous cultures and cosmic powers.

Conducive to meditation, healing and spiritual expression

📅 Spring (crisp, fresh weather and lots of spiritual conferences and healing seminars)
ℹ️ Sonora Tourism www.gotosonora.com

5 Mulu Caves

Sarawak, Borneo

Set deep with the rainforest of Sarawak's Gunung Mulu National Park, the Mulu Caves beg a zillion gushing superlatives. Dozens of caverns make up the complex cave system, from Wind Cave's breeze-filled calcite treasures to the imposing 107 km (66 mile)-long lime-stone of Clearwater Cave – the longest cave in Asia. Roaring crystalline rivers feed small, emerald streams while the sheer magnitude of Deer Cave defies description – but is reputed to be large enough to house five St. Paul's Cathedrals and over 20 Boeing 747 jumbo jets.

📅 Mar – Oct (driest season)
ℹ️ Mulu Caves Conservation Project www.mulucaves.org

6 Wreck Diving

Truk Lagoon, Micronesia

During World War II, campaigns against the Japanese deposited a couple hundred thousand tonnes of steel on the bottom of Truk Lagoon in Micronesia. Today, on resplendent coral growth, old Zero airplane fuselages and wing sections can still be found – providing scuba divers with one of the world's best wreck sites. The *Fujikawa Maru*'s hold still contains wartime ammunition, Dai Nippon beer bottles, stern guns and well-preserved telegraphs. Magnificent air compressors, a machine shop and a telephone booth can be clearly seen in the engine room of this World War II craft amidst a sea of anemones.

📅 Avoid the congestion of summer, early Mar is clear but crowd-free – and cheaper
ℹ️ Truk Lagoon www.truk-lagoon.com
Dive Truk Lagoon www.truk-lagoon-dive.com

Dive amongst sea anemones and Japanese airplane fuselages

Ice Golf World Championships | EUROPE

Uummannaq, Greenland

In March, temperatures in Uummannaq, Greenland settle at around -14°C (7°F), but occasionally dip down to -25°C (-13°F). However, despite the bitter cold (and biting wind chill) the sun shines brightly 600 km (373 miles) north of the Arctic Circle – just the weather for a game of golf. The World Ice Golf Championships has been a fixture in Uummannaq since 1997 and today golfers arrive from across the globe to do battle on a course that carves its way through ever-shifting icebergs with the marble-white 'greens' cut just a few hours before teeing off begins. Fluorescent orange balls help prevent losing a shot to a polar bear on this 9-hole par 35 course. However, nothing can prepare golfers for the challenge of the constantly moving pack-ice that allows new outcrops of ice to form.

23 Mar

ⓘ Greenland Tourism www.greenland.com

Tee off in -25°C (-13°F), north of the Arctic Circle

8 **Stiletto Run** | EUROPE

Join 150 spike-heeled fashionistas on a 100-metre (330-ft) dash

Amsterdam, Holland

Amsterdam's Stiletto Run takes place each year on the ultra-fashionable street of P.C. Hooftstraat, sending over 150 glamorous contestants tottering off in a 100 m (330 ft) dash with a 10,000 euro prize. Designed to encourage stiletto-wearing amongst the female business world, this bizarre event champions those women who are willing to suffer for their shoes. Rules dictate that heels should be no more than 1.5 centimetres (½ inch) wide and no less than 7 centimetres (2 ¾ inches) high.

23 Early Mar

ⓘ Stiletto Run www.glamour.nl/stilettorun

9 Holi

ASIA

Manipur, India

Manipur, in north-east India, celebrates the traditional Holi (Festival of Colours) by stretching festivities over six days from the full moon. Manipuris have given it added significance as a commemoration of the birth of Gauranga Mahaprabhu. Thousands of devotees flock to the Govindji Temple, the largest of Manipur's Vaishnavite shrines where a popular Manipuri folk dance, Thabal Chongba, is performed each day. For the Holi bonfire, a ceremonial hut is torched before coloured powders are thrown to ward off viral fever.

📅 3 days around full moon in Mar

ℹ️ India Tourism www.incredibleindia.org

10 Cherry Blossom Viewing

ASIA

Japan

Although strictly-speaking the term Hanami means "flower viewing" to the Japanese it means just one thing – a time to enjoy the arrival of cherry blossom. Cherry blossom viewing parties are a centuries-old tradition, ranging from couples sharing a simple snack under a lone tree to organised mass events. As the season only lasts around a fortnight in March or April, workers take time out from the office to marvel at the blooms. Typically, groups head to a park to unpack lunch boxes of sweet dumplings (dango) in a joyous celebration under intense clouds of delicate pink flora. Some trees are strung with fairy-lights for stunning night-time illumination. Prime spots in public places are reserved early in the morning – with Japan's most famous spots (such as Kyoto's Hirano Shrine and Tokyo's Ueno Park) prone to scuffles as crowds of picnickers converge.

📅 Mar – Apr

ℹ️ Japan Tourist Office www.jnto.go.jp

Picnic under blooms in a centuries-old Japanese tradition

11 Authentic African Bush Therapies | AFRICA

Botswana

Over 17 per cent of Botswana is designated protected parkland regions to conserve the fragile natural environment and its plants, trees, nuts, berries, seeds and fruit. Rains tend to start in October or November, and can persist until February – but in March, the early dry season, Botswana is at its most beautiful: nourished and sunny but not too hot. Some of the country's finest bush therapies are found close to the wildlife-rich 10,566 sq km (4,080 sq miles) Chobe National Park. The Chobe Chilwero Lodge boasts an enchanting setting amidst the abundant creatures and plants of the bush with panoramic views across rolling flood plains to Namibia. Africology spa therapies are based on ancient bush health philosophies and embody Africa's healing essences with Marula oil (Mother Nature's anti-oxidant), Rooibos extract (a natural anti-inflammatory), Locust Bean gum and sweet-smelling geranium.

📅 Mar

ⓘ Chobe Chilwero Spa www.chobechilwero.com
Botswana Tourism www.botswanatourism.co.bw

Chobe National Park is home to Africology pampering

12 Grand Bassin (Ganga Talao) | ASIA

Mauritius

Nestling in an extinct volcanic crater, the secluded Grand Bassin (Ganga Talao) is considered a sacred lake by Hindus, who make a pilgrimage to it every year for the Maha Shivaratri festival ('Siva's Great Night') when the Lord Siva is honoured (usually February - March). Believed to be filled with the waters of the holy Ganges of India, the Grand Bassin is as beautiful as it is spiritual with a temple, monument and lush, green meadows.

📅 Spring

ⓘ Mauritius Tourist Authority www.mauritius.net

13 Pasifika Festival

Auckland, New Zealand

As befitting the city with the largest Polynesian population in the world, Auckland celebrates its ethnic culture in a month-long programme of festivities centred on a two-day Pasifika Festival. While each year's programme follows a unique theme, the Western Springs Stadium is the main venue, playing host to a free Friday evening concert of top-name Polynesian musical talent. Come Saturday, the festival really kicks into gear as around a quarter-million visitors pack the stadium for a day of entertainment, handicraft markets, food stalls, costumes, dance and music. Some 10 different Pacific islands are represented in a blaze of colour: The Cook Islands, Fiji, Samoa, Tahiti, Tonga, Tokelau, Tuvalu, Kiribati, Niue, and Tangata Whenua. Village re-enactments depict traditional daily life and customs with demonstrations of drumming, weaving and wood carving together with Samoan tattooing. A wide range of ceremonies allow visitor participation, including a Tongan Kava ceremony with the traditional Kava drink and cooking workshops using exotic fruits, fish and vegetables to create mouth-watering Polynesian delicacies. Interactive exhibits in a purpose-built Families Area help storytellers bring the history of the Polynesian people to life amidst face-painters around the Children's Stage and a zillion brightly costumed masked dancers.

📅 3-day festival, part of a month-long cultural programme, mid-Mar

ℹ️ Auckland City Council www.aucklandcity.govt.nz

A colourful celebration of Polynesian tradition and culture

14 Wildfoods Festival | AUSTRALIA/PACIFIC

Hokitika, New Zealand

The clue for what lies in store at Hokitika Wildwoods is in the name – so expect a smorgasbord of bizarre epicurean delights. Since it launched in 1990, the festival has grown in stature and now lures 20,000 gastronomes with a curiosity for the weird and the wonderful to this tiny coastal town. Nibble on deep-fried ants, battered crickets, sushi-style slugs and cordon bleu sheep's eyes at this wacky extravaganza – a snapshot of the local area's gourmet bush tucker.

📅 Mar

ℹ Wildfoods Festival www.wildfoods.co.nz

Dine out on the weird, wonderful and truly bizarre

15 Zihuatanejo International Guitar Festival | NORTH AMERICA

Zihuatanejo Bay, Mexico

Each March the coastal town of Zihuatanejo, 210 km (130 miles) northwest of Acapulco, fills with the sound of nimble-fingered fretwork and furious strumming as the International Guitar Festival presents a week of performances in bars all over town. Guitar Fest represents a wide array of genres, from flamenco, classical and blues to folk and jazz.

On the final day,

free-flowing jam sessions dominate the downtown district, followed by free open-air gigs in the main plaza and esplanade.

📅 1-week, late Mar

ℹ Zihuatanejo International Guitar Fest www.zihuafest.info
Mexico Tourist Board www.visitmexico.com

16 Ice Cricket | EUROPE

Estonia

On an ice-frosted pitch with a snowy outfield, 12 brave souls play ice cricket to six-a-side rules on rugged Estonian terrain. During the round-robin Ice Cricket tournament, frost-bite is a hazard for bowlers while batters can add an few extra runs if they manage to hit a wild moose or cross-country skier. The venue, Tallinn's Harku boating lake, freezes rapidly in early January to provide a solid, flat wicket where temperatures plummet to -25°C (-13°F). Fluffy, fresh snowfall is ideal for those rolling catches before any signs of melting slush, end of March.

📅 Jan – Mar

ℹ Real Ice Cricket www.realicecricket.co.uk
Estonia Tourism www.visitestonia.com

17 St Patrick's Day

Dublin, Ireland

Just a few decades ago, St Patrick's Day was a relatively quiet day in Ireland. As a religious holiday, the pubs were closed. No one dyed anything green. Most Dubliners attended Mass, ate a big meal with family and friends – and enjoyed a couple of jars at home. Today, over 70 million people worldwide claim Irish heritage – and St Patrick's Day has become a byword for Guinness-fuelled merry-making. St Patrick's Day falls right in the middle of Lent – traditionally a time of restraint and fasting. However, these rules have always been bent on March 17th with a shared pint (or two) after mass. When emptying the pota Pádraig, "Patrick's Pot", the final drink is decorated with a shamrock – before being drowned in whiskey and flung over the left shoulder for good luck. Every year Dublin's St Patrick's Festival involves over 4,000 performers in the celebrating of everything Irish – from the flag, the culture, the humour and the music to the food and the language – and lots of the black stuff in pints. People fly in from all over the world to honour their Irish ancestry joining several thousand Dublin residents and pilgrims from all over Ireland – not forgetting the crowds of would-be Paddies who wish they had Irish blood.

📅 5 days ending on the Mar 17th

ⓘ St Patrick's Festival www.stpatricksday.ie
  Dublin Tourist Board www.visitdublin.com

Green dye, shamrocks, Irish flags and a zillion pints of Guinness

18 The Ancient Souks of Old Aleppo | ASIA

Haggle in backstreet bazaars of the oldest continuously-inhabited trading cities

Syria

In the Ottoman age, Syria's second city Aleppo welcomed merchants from Turkey, France and England to covered bazaars. Located 350 km (218 miles) north of Damascus, Aleppo is one of the world's oldest continuously inhabited cities and remains a lively trading hub as shoppers haggle over every conceivable article be it rolls of carpet, silks, spices, fruits, textiles or soap. Shakespeare made mention of Aleppo's exotic trading charms in *Macbeth* and *Othello* and artisans still craft their wares in a crowded, energetic marketplace to the delicious aromas of bubbling lentil soup, samaka harra and freshly-cooked sesame muffins. The city's famous handmade soap is dried November to March before being piled high in slabs in the souk, making March a good month to visit.

📅 Mar (for when Aleppo's hand-cut soap gets to market)

ℹ️ Syria Tourist Office www.syriatourism.org

19 Caribou Carnival | NORTH AMERICA

Yellowknife, Canada

Over 50 years ago Yellowknife's Caribou Carnival began as an annual gathering of trappers proving their prowess. Men competed by proving their ability to survive the harshest winters – skills that remain important in Yellowknife today. Today, locals honour springtime in an array of cultural celebrations that reflect Yellowknife's caribou herds and mining heritage in a wilderness region on the northern shores of Great Slave Lake – a gateway to the Arctic.

📅 Last week of Mar

ℹ️ Canada Tourist Office www.canada.travel

20 World Marbles Championship | EUROPE

Tinsley Green, England

Around 20 teams compete in the World Marbles Championship in Tinsley Green, Sussex, England representing nations as far flung as the Czech Republic and Australia. The game of marbles has been enjoyed by children for generations, but don't be fooled into thinking that this sporting competition is a playground pastime – it's an adult pursuit that has transformed the art of flicking glass balls into a fiercely fought battle. With ritualistic devotion, a purpose-designed six foot concrete ring in the shadow of Gatwick airport is swept and the sand raked. Forty-nine marbles are then placed in the ring with ceremonial precision. Players get a point for each marble they are able to knock out of the ring with their Tolley (a shooting marble). The first team to reach 25 points wins.

Marbles has been played in Sussex for centuries but the current championships were launched at the Greyhound Inn in 1932. Tales of legendary local mibsters (marble practitioners) are manifold and ancient marble folklore goes as far back as Elizabethan times. The game has its own entrenched and unforgivingly strict rules. It also boasts a curious vocabulary littered with nose drop, fudging, hunching, histing, cabbaging and knuckling down.

Thousands of spectators converge on Tinsley Green each year on Good Friday including a large contingent of fans from Germany and Australia – both formidable competitive forces in the marble world's most gruelling open competition. Offbeat it may be, but a joke it isn't: with each team fully prepped and primed with the cup in its sights.

📅 Good Friday (Easter Weekend)
❶ British Marbles Board of Control marblesam@hotmail.com Tel: 01403 730602

21 Nau Roz, Afghan New Year | ASIA

Mazar e Sharif, Afghanistan

Though celebrated country-wide, Afghanistan's largest festival is synonymous with Mazar e Sharif, where celebrations can stretch to 10 days – or more. Traditionally a time when honours are bestowed on artists and farmers, Nau Roz is famous for its picnics, music and dancing in the parks. Men and boys raise the so called 'holy pole' to gauge the prosperity of the upcoming year while New Year festivities herald the reawakening of nature – flinging their doors and windows wide to let in the fresh air of spring.

📅 Jan – Mar, depending on Islamic calendar
❶ Travel Afghanistan www.travelafghanistan.co.uk

22 Abu Dhabi Music and Arts Festival | ASIA

United Arab Emirates

In just a few years, Abu Dhabi's Music and Arts Festival has established itself as the region's premier international artistic gathering, attracting big names such as the Bolshoi Ballet and the London Philharmonic Orchestra – to name just a few. For 12 days, this celebration of music, dance and art brings together artists from Western and Eastern cultures to the marble and gilded Emirates Palace – one of the most elegant and expensive hotels ever built and a ritzy prelude to Saadiyat Island and its new performing-arts centre designed by Zaha Hadid.

23 2 weeks, mid-Mar 'til Apr

❶ Abu Dhabi Arts Festival www.admafestival.com
Abu Dhabi Tourism www.visitabudhabi.ae

23 Giant Pandas | ASIA

Wolong Nature Reserve, China

Pregnant once a year, female giant pandas conceive in spring and give birth between 95 and 160 days later. Young are pink, sparsely haired, blind and helpless. The size of a hotdog, each weighs around 150 g (5 oz). After a week, dark patches begin to appear near the eyes and ears while the skin on their legs and backs begins to darken. Baby pandas' eyes open after about a month with crawling two to three months later. Giant pandas are cubs until two years old. At the Wolong Nature Reserve in China, the young of this endangered species can be visited March-Nov, drawing people from all over China – and the world to view.

23 Mar – Nov

❶ China National Tourist Office www.cnto.org
Wolong Nature Reserve www.chinawolong.com

24 Tayrona National Park | SOUTH AMERICA

Colombia

As the month of March comes to an end, the creeper-clad forest of Tayrona National Park quenches its thirst on a daily light sprinkling of rain. Flowers and leaves unfurl in a fresh, new explosion of colour amidst a dense rainforest that is home to wild pigs, sloth, spider-monkeys, lizards, parrots and snakes. Explore pre-Hispanic trails on horseback, by mule or on foot to spot spider webs the size of table cloths stretched from tree-to-tree. Journey around a spit that links silver sand beaches hemmed by coconut trees.

23 End Mar

❶ www.minicomercio.gov.co

25 Vanilla Pollination | NORTH AMERICA

Papantla, Mexico

Arrive in Papantla during pollination season (late March - early April) and the town's small family-run vanilla farms are a buzz of excitement and yellow orchid blooms. Hear the piercing call of the native Totonac flute and imbibe the fragrant perfume of fresh vanilla in this enchanting settlement in the foothills of the Sierra Madre Oriental. Abundant vanilla crops lend Papantla the nickname: 'La ciudad que perfuma al mundo' – meaning the city that perfumes the world. Flowers bloom just once a year, closing after pollination to form a vanilla pod.

Mar (pollination time)

Mexico Tourist Board www.visitmexico.com

26 Belly Dancing (Göbek Atmak) | EUROPE

Istanbul, Turkey

Belly dancing has been a part of Istanbul's culture for centuries. Called *göbek atmak* in Turkish (meaning 'tossing the belly button'), the dance has its roots in ancient fertility rituals when women danced for the benefit of other women. At Istanbul's premier belly dancing venue Sultana's, spectators can learn belly dancing, watch some of Turkey's finest dancers and enjoy the hypnotic Middle Eastern music. Arrive in March to experience the city's heady blossom.

Mar (the city is rich in a heady blossom and sprouting green shoots)

Turkey Tourism www.tourismturkey.org

An intoxicating age-old fertility ritual

27 Godwit Migration | AUSTRALIA/PACIFIC

New Zealand

After spending their winters in New Zealand the Bar-Tailed Godwit turn their attention to breeding in Alaska. To bolster energy-levels ahead of this mammoth trip, the birds feed heavily on shellfish and molluscs in mud-flats on the south side of the Firth of Thames. As the godwits arrive the people of the town of Miranda prepare for the Departure of the Birds festival in late March – an event that draws hundreds to view the flocks poised to migrate.

Mar

www.newzealand.com

28 Nyepi

Bali, Indonesia

In sharp contrast with the boisterous revelry associated with the Western New Year, the Balinese welcome their New Year in the tranquillity of meditative silence. Called Nyepi, the day follows the dark moon of the spring equinox in which the Balinese restore the balance of nature in their lives. At the stroke of midnight, all of Bali retreats into quietude for 24 hours – airports close, shops shut and every street lamp is switched off. Roads are empty and entire towns and villages deserted as Bali is plunged into darkness. En mass, Hindus turn their backs on work, travel, the telephone, TV, games, conversation and sex in a collective attempt to purify the island through meditation to realign the forces of evil and good.

The principles of Nyepi are ancient and relate to the earth, moon and sun at their nearest proximity - with the sun being directly above the equator, moving from the southern to the northern hemisphere. On this day Yama (the 'lord of hell') is believed to throw open his gates to let a horde of devils wreak potential havoc. In preparedness, the Balinese erect altars in strategic positions and by each shrine, they leave delicious offerings to lure the devils into the realm of the Brahman high priests who wait for the evil spirits with spells and mantras at the ready. Ahead of the call for silence, people take to the streets in a rowdy procession (Tawur Kesanga) of grotesque papier mache monsters and banging gongs, clashing cymbals and beating drums. Once all latent demons have been roused and exorcised, the paper monsters are set ablaze to symbolize the retreat of evil from the island - before the sun sets and silence begins. On the day after Nyepi, the festival of Ngembak Geni is a chance for each Hindu to look inward and ask

A comtemplative period of introspection as Bali is plunged into darkness

"how can I be better?" Visits to friends, family and neighbours are commonplace to welcome a new year – and a new start.

25 Bali's Lunar New Year (Mar - Apr)

❶ Indonesia Tourism www.my-indonesia.info

29 Cape Epic | AFRICA

South Africa

Only the tough, insane or ill-advised seriously consider the Cape Epic mountain bike race from Knysna to Cape Town across a challenging 901 km (560 mile) route over several days. Yet over 800 entrants do – despite the threat of fatigue, saddle sores and cramp – and slog it out across some of South Africa's finest scenery of mountains, indigenous forests and semi-desert Karoo in this late March - early April event, where 8 out of 10 riders require medical attention before crossing the finishing line.

📅 1 week, Mar
ℹ Cape Epic www.cape-epic.com
   Cape Town Tourism www.capetown.travel

Only two out of ten riders make it back without medical help

30 Wine-tasting | SOUTH AMERICA

Vendimia, Isla de Maipo, Chile

Spring is a time when local wine producers celebrate the fruits of their labour. In the last weekend in March, crowds start gathering in the early morning on the Plaza de Marmas in Isla de Maipo for one of the best Wine Festivals in Chile. Only 40 minutes from Santiago, the Vendimia on the Isla de Maipo draws over 17,000 people for wild grape-crushing dances, folkloric displays, live music and salsa together with lots of wine-tasting.

📅 Last weekend in Mar
ℹ Chile Tourist Board www.visit-chile.org
   Wines of Chile www.winesofchile.org

31 Festival of the North | ASIA

Murmansk, Russia

Participants from all over Eastern Europe arrive in the Russian Lapland region for the Festival of the North each March when the bright sunshine and ultra-low temperatures ensure gorgeous conditions for snow sports. With cross-country races, biathlons, downhill skiing, figure skating and ice hockey, the festival also includes reindeer team racing, group parachute jumps and a cold-water swimming event. However, it is the finale that draws the crowds to Murmansk – a spectacular 50 km (31 mile) ski marathon in Cozy Valley (Dolina Uyuta) that has been run since 1934.

📅 Varies, Mar
ℹ Russia Tourism visitrussia.org.uk

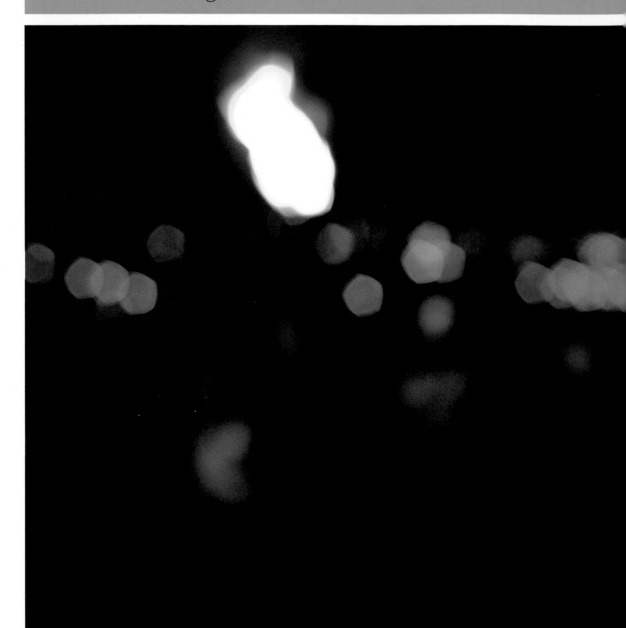

April

1 Melbourne Comedy Festival
AUSTRALIA/PACIFIC

Australia

As Australia's comedy capital, Melbourne plays host to the International Comedy Festival, one of the three largest comedy festivals in the world, alongside the Edinburgh Festival Fringe and Montreal's Just for Laughs. Launched in 1987 by Barry Humphries and Peter Cook, Melbourne's annual comedy fest boasts a powerful program of stand-up, improvisation, cabaret, street theatre, film, television and radio.

Running for three-and-a-half side-splitting weeks, the festival showcases and celebrates top Aussie and international comic talent.

📅 1 month, Apr

ℹ Melbourne International Comedy Festival
www.comedyfestival.com.au
Melbourne Tourism www.visitmelbourne.com

2 Teotihuacan Pyramids
NORTH AMERICA

Mexico

The Teotihuacan Pyramids are two of the world's three largest pyramids. The Pyramid of the Sun and Calle de los Muertos (Street of the Dead) boast some magnificent original characteristics and there are amazingly well-preserved murals, butterfly-shaped sculptures and serpents in the Temple of Quetzalcoatl. Altitude can hinder exploration in the

oppressive mid-summer heat so arrive early morning in March – June in order to walk and climb this holy Aztec site.

📅 Year round, but better in the spring

ℹ Mexico Cultural Tours www.mexicoculturaltours.com
Mexico Tourism www.visitmexico.com

3 Rattlesnake Hunt
NORTH AMERICA

Waurika, Oklahoma, USA

While most people avoid rattlesnakes at all costs, Oklahoma festivals positively encourage people to look for them. Home to a thriving rattlesnake population, Oklahoma runs rattlesnake roundups January to July each year, with April the peak month for rattler encounters. Scheduled on alternating weekends, snakehunts take place in Okeene (west), Waynoka (north-west), Waurika, Apache and

Mangum (south-west) with events that include snake handling and live rattlesnake pits. Food stalls are not for the squeamish with snake-burgers, deep-fried rattler snacks and cured snake meat.

📅 Apr 3 days

ℹ Waurika Oklahoma Rattlesnake Hunt
www.rattlesnakehunt.com

A transparent ledge over a death-defying 1,220 metre (4,000 ft) drop

4 **Grand Canyon Skywalk** | NORTH AMERICA

Nevada, USA

Set in striking amber-coloured rock, Nevada's Skywalk provides a terrifying walk out over a 20 m (65 ft) transparent death-defying protrusion that juts out over a gasp-inducing 1,220 m (4,000 ft)- drop high above a canyon.

Reached by a two-hour drive from Vegas, the horseshoe-shaped walkway has been built to exacting standards. Only 120 people are allowed on it at any time, considerably less than the 820 it can comfortably support. It can also cope with an 8.0-magnitude earthquake within 80 km (50 miles). However, while it may be calibrated to cope with a weight of 70 tons and resist wind speeds in excess of 160 kph (100 mph), it wobbles and creaks in a most disconcerting way that can turn gentle anxiety into mild panic. Skywalk is engineered to withstand extreme gusts, but even adrenaline-freaks may want to give it a miss in the windiest months. Opt for March or April to avoid the worst of the region's dust storms and the perilous midair trembles they inflict.

Dozens of 2 m (6 ft) deep beams are anchored in place by 108 steel supports driven 12 m (40 ft) into the rock – although it is just a 10 cm (4 in) piece of glass (made of five extra-tough layers) that separates visitors from the gravitational consequences of a plummet. Shoulder-height walls are glass too, though the roof is open. Thrill-seekers are drawn to the Skywalk for the heart-in-mouth experience it offers. As you step over the void and look down to the distant, jagged rocks of the valley floor, your stomach is guaranteed to turn somersaults . To be so high, unaided over hundreds of multi-layered strata is unnatural, weird and horrifying, but one heck of a buzz.

📅 Mar - Apr (to avoid dust storms and high winds)
ℹ️ Grand Canyon Skywalk www.grandcanyonskywalk.com

5 Tracking Mountain Gorillas | AFRICA

Southwest Uganda

As the largest and rarest of the primates, the gorilla can weigh up to 200 kg (440 lbs) and grow to 1.8 m (6 ft) in height. In Uganda this mainly ground-dwelling species inhabit the region's open canopy forests – and their grunts, barks, screeches and chest beating can often be heard for great distances. Mountain gorillas have a fairly limited home range, making them easier to track and habituate for tourism and research. In spring, the sub-tropical Virunga Mountains along the south-west Ugandan border are wet and quiet – and a great time to see these giants amongst broad-leaved banana plants.

Mar – early May

Gorilla Safaris www.gorilla-safaris.co.ug

Uganda Gorilla Safari Tours
www.ugandagorillasafaritours.com

Uganda Tourism www.visituganda.com

Mountain gorillas inhabit Uganda's lush, green, open canopy forests

6 Motorcycle Skijoring | EUROPE

Beskydy Mountains, Czech Republic

In the Czech Republic, motorcycle skijoring involves being pulled along on skis by a full-throttle Honda XR 400 trail motorbike, rather than the customary dogs. As part of a frontier range that run from north to south, Beskydy Mountains boast an elevation of around 1,000 m (3,280 ft) above sea level. Long, rolling hillsides covered by almost continuous snow cover during a long, cold winter make the region ideal for cross-country pursuits, such as skiing, sledding and motorcycle skijoring. Expect early flurries in November with ground cover 'til early April.

Mid – Nov to early Apr

Czech Republic Tourism www.czechtourism.com

7 Mount Vesuvius

Naples, Italy

Curving seductively for about 32 km (20 miles), the Bay of Naples is rich in poignant ruins, magma crusts, fumaroles and craters. Towering above it all is Mount Vesuvius, one of the most dangerous volcanoes on earth. Steep trails up to a stream-cloaked summit at 1,281 m (4,200 ft) lead through gnarled lava fields to a 500 m (1,640 ft)-wide gaping chasm; dark, eerie and ringed with silver-grey ash. Quite apart from its most dramatic outburst in AD79, Vesuvius has erupted many times and is likely to erupt again. On April 7, 1906 clouds of lava ash spewed out across Naples to heights of 13 km (8 miles), rivers of molten rock razed it to the ground – and the eruption climaxed with lava fountains and earthquakes.

📅 7th Apr (anniversary of 1906 eruption that razed Naples to the ground)

ℹ️ Mount Vesuvius National Park www.vesuviopark.it
Vesuvio Guide www.vesuviotour.com

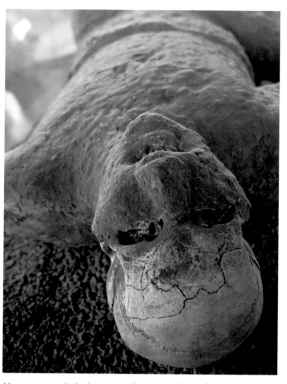

Magma-encrusted ruins are a poignant reminder of this day in 1906

8 Spring in Petra

Jordan

Petra enjoys a glorious period of fresh, cool(ish) breezes from January to early May. As Jordan's most picturesque archaeological treasure, the UNESCO World Heritage Site doesn't disappoint those prepared to explore its narrow streets. There is much to see in the former capital city of the Arabic Nabatean tribe at the convergence of three ancient trade routes – a rose-stone settlement

rediscovered in 1812. Enter a skinny alleyway carved through towering rock to emerge in a history-steeped wonderland tinged with pink where rough steps lead to the altars of the High Place of Sacrifice and stunning mountain views.

📅 Mar – Apr
ℹ️ Jordan Tourism Authority www.visitjordan.com

9 Walking the Cinque Terre

EUROPE

Italy

In early April, walkers are thin on the ground along the knitted mesh of trails in Italy's Cinque Terre ("five lands") despite pleasing weather. Take the rugged Seniero Azzuro coastal path to soak up incredible views of sheltered coves and waves crashing over breakwaters on rocky headlands. Pirates once ranged the coast, so the 11 km (9 mile) trail is rich in legends of plunder and treasure. Explore the five charming hillside villages strung out along this breathtaking UNESCO site where dramatic vine-cloaked slopes tumble sea-wards amidst vertical cliffs and trickling creeks.

🗓 Spring

ℹ Cinque Terre Tourism www.cinqueterre.it

10 Bathe in the Dead Sea

ASIA

Jordan

Believed to be the ancient site of five biblical cities (Sodom, Admah, Zebouin, Gomorrah and Zoar) deep in the Jordan Valley 55 km (34 miles) southeast of Amman, the Dead Sea is one of the most spectacular natural and holy landscapes on Earth. As the planet's lowest body of water and the world's richest source of natural salts, its unique chemical composition has attracted visitors for thousands of years. Fed by numerous incoming rivers, the Dead Sea is devoid of life due to an extremely high saline content that is believed to boast curative powers – over 35 minerals have been indentified in its waters. Once a convergence point for royalty, merchants, emperors and prophets, the Dead Sea is surrounded by a surreal terrain that boasts sunsets of fire-burst hues. A rock-hewn marker indicates "Sea Level", but the Dead Sea itself is a further descent of some 400 m (1,310 ft). Most visitors delight in the buoyancy it offers, reclining effortlessly on the soothing waters whilst reading a newspaper – the water is 10 times saltier than sea water. On the first or second Friday in April, this bobbing-cork position affords unbeatable views of the Dead Sea Marathon – Jordan's "run to the lowest point on Earth".

Bouyant bathing in the world's lowest body of water

🗓 Arrive in time for the Dead Sea Marathon, mid-Apr

ℹ Jordan Tourist Board www.visitjordan.com

11 Two Oceans Marathon

Cape Town, South Africa

Though it is often described as "The World's Most Beautiful Marathon", Cape Town's Two Ocean's slog is no scenic stroll. Entrants happily admit they are "self-respecting masochists" who "enjoy torture on a spectacular backdrop". With 26,000 participants lining up on the starting line on the Saturday of Easter Weekend, the event has become something of an institution since the first marathon in 1970. It offers a half marathon (21 km (13 mile)) and a number of fun run options (8 km (5 mile), 5 km (3 mile) and 2.5 km (1.5 mile)) together with the ultra (56 km (35 mile)) marathon - longer than the standard marathon route. The course traverses the Table Mountain National Park - a Natural World Heritage Site - and provides a gruelling test of fitness for both the elite and amateur runner. Easter celebrations add an air of festivity to the city as it grinds to a halt to cheer the runners on.

📅 Easter Weekend (Saturday)

ⓘ Two Oceans Marathon www.twooceansmarathon.org.za

A gruelling test of grit and determination along a 56 km (35 mile) course over Easter weekend

12 Le Mat Snake Festival

Hanoi, Vietnam

According to legend, the people of Le Mat hamlet in Viet Hung village about 7 km (4 miles) from downtown Hanoi have a special talent for catching snakes. In ancient times, a princess was attacked by a mammoth snake while boating on the Red River. Her life was saved when a young man fought off the serpent – and then went on to found the settlement of Le Mat. Today, the festival dedicated to the snake-slaying might of Le Mat's ancestor centres on a water procession from the river to his temple. Coinciding with the May full moon, the annual festival draws 13 elders from surrounding villagers who bring 13 trays of food above their heads to the communal house. Snake sculptures made of bamboo and cloth form the centrepiece of the pageant. Colourful snake dances simulate the triumph with cups of (non-poisonous) snake venom wine drunk to celebrate this auspicious day. Le Mat is said to have practised snake trading and slaying for over 900 years, a skill handed down from generation to generation.

🗓 23rd day of the 3rd lunar month (Apr)

❶ Vietnam Tourism www.vietnamtourism.com

Snake sculptures, dances and venom commemorate the legend of an auspicious slaying of a serpent

13 NASA Launch

Space Coast, USA

Watching a NASA space launch is exciting enough on TV, but nothing compares with an up-close frontline view. The Kennedy Space Station east of Orlando is America's busiest rocket and shuttle launch facility, so the spectacle involves the thunderous ascent of massive rockets carrying satellites, Martian rovers, planetary explorers and more. Space operations require huge amounts of unpopulated land because of noise and safety issues. NASA has put this land to good effect by designating it a wildlife refuge – the road that leads to the launch pad mixes exciting technology with wild manatees, nesting eagles and basking alligators amidst rivers, swamp and forests.

Over more than 30 years, the Kennedy Space Centre has welcomed millions of spectators to the venue of such landmark missions as Apollo 11's interplanetary jaunt to the moon. Today, most visitors get a chance to witness STS or Space shuttle (on launch complex 39, pads A & B); Atlas V (complex 41); Delta II Space Launch (complex 17 pads A & B) and Delta IV (complex 37) – but all sorts of top-notch missions are imminent. Tours tell the story of how the United States built a space program that launched men to the Moon while exhibits demonstrate the impact of orbited satellites and how probes in distant space can solve age-old cosmic mysteries. Tickets are sold online for a range of viewing packages – the best option offers access to the closest public viewing gallery - the NASA Causeway (only NASA officials can get any closer than this). Anticipation reaches fever pitch at the sound of the countdown over the PA system with cheers, tears and audible gasps as a flame-lit thrusting roar powers the rocket into the sky. To avoid a disappointing bad-weather launch cancellation, give the hurricane season (June – November) a miss.

Witness the thrilling spectacle of an intergalactic space rocket

📅 Dec – May is launching season

ℹ NASA www.nasa.gov

14 Boun Pi Mai, Laotian New Year | ASIA

Luang Pra Bang, Laos

Though the Gregorian calendar applies officially in Laos, many communities follow the Lunar Calendar. New Year (Pi Mai) is celebrated each year in April, between 14th and 16th, with pre-festival rituals on the 13th. Before Pi Mai, Buddha images are taken out of the temples for cleansing with scented water. As the water splashes off the images, it is gathered up in vessels and taken home for use in purification rituals with friends and relatives. Pi Mai is one of the best times to visit Laos as the sun is hot and the famous water fights are a source of fun and frivolity. Ceremonies take place in almost all temples but the UNESCO-heritage town of Luang Pra Bang is renowned for its colourful vibrancy and cultural traditions.

📅 Apr, between 14th and 16th, with pre-festival rituals on the 13th

ℹ Laos National Tourism Authority www.tourismlaos.gov.la

15 Merrie Monarch Hula Festival | NORTH AMERICA

Hilo, Hawaii

For almost 50 years the week-long Merrie Monarch Festival has honoured Hawaii's ancient tradition of the hula dance. Named after King David Kalakaua, who is beloved for reviving hula in the late 19th century, after decades of disapproval by Christian missionaries, the festival involves a ritual at the rim of Kilauea Crater to honour fire goddess Pele. A centre stage wows the crowds with hula demonstrations while a garland-strewn parade proudly promotes the belief systems of ancient Hawaii. Thousands arrive for the festival's three-day hula and vibrant luau (Hawaiian party) in which music and dance provide a powerful means of sharing mythic tales of tragic lovers, comic animals and petulant gods.

📅 3-days, Apr

ℹ Merrie Monarch Festival www.merriemonarchfestival.org

16 St Lazaru Procession | EUROPE

Larnaca, Cyprus

Eight days before the Greek Orthodox celebration of Easter, the townspeople of Larnaca celebrate the feast day of their patron saint, St Lazarus. The gilded icon of Saint Lazarus is held aloft at the front of a lively parade through Larnaca's streets, led by the priest of the Church of St Lazarus. After Jesus raised Saint Lazarus from the dead he was ordained the Bishop of Kition (Larnaca's ancient name) by Saints Barnabas and Paul.

📅 Eight days before the Greek Orthodox celebration of Easter

ℹ Cyprus Tourism www.visitcyprus.com

17 London Marathon

London, England

When the London Marathon was first run in 1981 few believed it would become the biggest charity fund-raising marathon on the planet with more than 75 per cent of the entrants raising money – a combined total of over £300 million. One of the top five international marathons run over the traditional distance of 42.195 km (26 miles and 385 yards), the April event boasts a carnival atmosphere quite unlike any other marathon with thousands of outlandish costume-clad runners – fluffy chickens, two-man pantomime horses, super-heroes and cows in luminous spandex, not to mention heavyweight deep-sea diving gear. Runners follow a route in two hemispheres – the East and the West – as the course crosses the Prime Meridian in Greenwich. A small number of male runners, known as the "Ever Presents", have completed all the London Marathons.

📅 Sunday, mid – late Apr (to avoid Easter)

ℹ️ London Marathon www.london-marathon.co.uk

Costume-clad runners do battle with the athletic elite

18 Nakizumo (Crying Sumo for Babies)

Tokyo, Japan

According to an old Japanese proverb, babies with a piercing cry grow up to be healthy – a theory that is put to the test in the 400-year-old Crying Sumo (Nakizumo) festival. Celebrated across Japan, Nakizumo is believed to also drive away evil spirits. More than 200 babies take part in Tokyo's annual event at the Sensoji temple where hulking sumo wrestlers gently shake the infants in a bid to see how powerfully they can wail. To ensure their cries are

closer to heaven, the sumo hold the babies up high as they bawl. Some babies refuse to make a peep despite the encouragement of judges who whisper "nake, nake (cry, cry)". Others laugh as the mammoth sumo attempt to evoke tears with growls and grimaces.

📅 Sunday, Apr

ℹ️ Japan National Tourist Office www.jnto.go.jp

19 Reef Diving | SOUTH AMERICA

Belize

As the home of the longest barrier reef in the Western Hemisphere and the second longest on the planet, Belize is a paradise for scuba divers and snorkelers. For the ultimate water clarity, arrive mid-March to May when visibility of up to 30 m (100 ft) allows unbeatable underwater views of colourful sponges, corals and other reef species. This is also the time when Belize's translucent waters are home to migratory whale sharks – the world's largest fish at up to 18 m (60 ft) in length. These harmless filter feeders congregate off the southern coast on a reef cut called Gladden Spit – one of the few places in the world where scuba divers have a real chance of spotting and swimming with these friendly and inquisitive giants. Weighing in excess of 15 tons, whale sharks typically migrate three days before and seven days after a full moon, during the spring month during a lunar cycle in which millions of snappers mate and spawn. Though intimidating in size, these gentle beasts avoid confrontation. As the bubbles from a diver's regulator look like snapper eggs, it is not uncommon for whale sharks to swim up close (almost eye-to-eye) out of curiosity and hunger, though they pose no threat.

📅 Year-round, though at its most clear Mar – May when whale sharks can be spotted

ℹ️ Belize Tourism Organisation www.travelbelize.org

20 Elephant Races | ASIA

Buon Don, Vietnam

Throughout Vietnam, the Dac Lac province is synonymous with elephants and is frequented year-round for its elephant rides, tug-of-wars, football matches and swimming competitions. However, it is the Elephant Race in the highland district of Buon Don that draws the biggest crowds – a rush of people charge to the starting line once they hear the drum beat and clanging gongs that herald the start of a race. Around 10 elephants take part, each ridden by two 'jockeys' - one for speed and one for navigation. The pace is surprisingly fast thanks their special pre-race diet of bananas, papayas and sugar cane.

📅 Apr, when the temperature is cool

ℹ️ Sri Lanka Tourism www.srilankatourism.org

Witness elephant tug-of-wars and sprints in Buon Don

21 Blue Metropolis Literary Festival | NORTH AMERICA

Montreal, Canada

Since ancient times, travel – be it cycling, sailing, running, rowing or taking an intergalactic jaunt - has been a theme for writers, from Cevantes, Dante and Samuel Johnson to Jules Verne and Proust. At the Blue Metropolis International Literary Festival, writers gather to discuss the places that have inspired them – whether in memory or imagination. Collective nouns are among the most vivid words in language (think exaltation of larks and a pandemonium of parrots), so they decided to call themselves "a Blue Metropolis of writers". Today, the world's first multilingual literary festival attracts over 350 writers, translators, journalists and publishers to a five-day literary party.

📅 5 days in Apr
ℹ Blue Metropolis International Literary Festival
  bluemetropolis.org

22 Beat the Ballot | EUROPE

St Andrews Old Course, Scotland

As the self-proclaimed 'Home of Golf', St Andrews has welcomed golfers for more than six centuries, from Old Tom Morris and Bobby Jones to Jack Nicklaus and Tiger Woods. To walk the prestigious fairways, golfers must enter a ballot. A whispered prayer to the site's religious relics by the West Bay is a common ritual. But not even this attempt to prompt a miracle can 'magic up' a tee-time at this hugely oversubscribed course. Simply hand in a card or call the ballot line by 2pm to take a punt. Is there a lucky month? Not according to course officials, though the locals swear you've more chance of winning a ballot in April and May.

📅 Apr - May
ℹ St Andrews Golf www.standrews.org.uk

Beat the ballot at the world's so-called 'Home of Golf'

23 Festival de la Leyenda Vallenata | SOUTH AMERICA

Valledupar, Colombia

Each year in April, many thousands of devotees of Colombia's ever-popular Vallenato music flock to the city of Valledupar for the Festival de la Leyenda Vallenata. Meaning "born in the valley", Vallenato is the traditional working man's music of the Atlantic Coast: a mix of upbeat percussion and folksy, bouncy accordion refrains. Since its inception in 1968, the festival has grown into Colombia's largest folk music event. Over five long days of partying and feasting, the rhythms of merengue, paseo, puya and son are celebrated to the max.

23 5 days, late Apr

❶ Festival de la Leyenda Vallenata www.festivalvallenato.com

Bouncy accordion refrains typify Colombia's Vallenato music

24 Battle of the Moors and Christians | EUROPE

Alcoy, Valencia, Spain

Every year, communities throughout Southern Spain celebrate the Spanish re-conquest of the Iberian Peninsula from the Moors. By far the biggest, most fervent re-enactment is in Alcoy, 45 km (28 miles) north of Alicante. A three-day festival begins with costumed parades followed next day by religious services and celebrations of St. Georges Day. After a ceremonial procession through the town a firework display illuminates the skies and effigies are burned on huge bonfires. On the final day of the festival, the townsfolk stage a bloody battle, complete with a papier-mâché castle in the main square – a piece of high drama that commemorates a battle in 1276. Almost unchanged in 700 years, proceedings centre on combat between troops led by the Christian ruler and the Moorish captain Al Athrak. The Moors seize the castle in the morning, the Christians regain control in the afternoon – and the battle is won.

23 Late Apr, 3 days

❶ Valencia Tourist Office www.turisvalencia.es

25 Segway

Washington D.C., USA

April brings near-perfect weather to Washington DC where sightseeing the city using a futuristic, self-propelled contraption is all the rage. The Segway PT (personal transporter) has been hailed a pedestrian speed-freak's friend: a gliding, spinning self-balancing stand-up scooter that whizzes around the capitol's iconic monuments scattering pigeons.

Tours begin with an introduction and training session on which levers, knobs and handlebars are twiddled. Within a few minutes, most riders can roll forwards and backwards and turn in a complete circle. Twisting the handlebar to the left produces a pirouetting twirl. The learning curve may be steep, but it's mercifully brief. The nimble Segway is designed to mirror the human body's mechanics as it hurls itself around ornamental fountains and charges along sidewalks. Shifting stance acts as a rudder while a slick, gliding action gives the appearance of effortless ease. Without brakes, stopping is precarious – something that George W. Bush famously discovered when he slipped off a PT in the full glare of the world's media in 2003.

Whiz around the US capital on a personal transporter

🗓 Year-round, but Apr has perfect weather
ℹ City Segway Tours www.citysegwaytours.com
   Washington DC Tourism www.washington.org

26 Olive Throwing

Mora, Spain

For two solid days, the small town of Mora, 24 km (15 miles) south-east of Toledo, lets its hair down over the last weekend in April in joyous celebration of the abundant local olive groves. Colourful parades, bull running, folk-dancing and the crowning of the olive queen attract thousands to the Fiesta de Olivo (Olive Festival). The olive throwing contest is the most exuberant component of the weekend with much carousing and merriment late into the night.

🗓 3rd Sunday in Apr
ℹ Olive Festival www.fiestadelolivo.es

27 North Carolina Pickle Festival | NORTH AMERICA

North Carolina, USA

According to the devotees behind North Carolina's Pickle Festival, the humble acetic acid-preserved cucumber dates back to around 2030BC. Today, pickle juice (vinegar to you or I) is considered a first-rate sore throat remedy while old wives tales swear by pickles as a cure for gout. Now approaching its 25th year, the North Carolina Pickle Festival sings the praises of the simple pickle at a pickle farm in leafy

Mount Olive. Aside from traditional fare, you'll find all sorts of pickle-related activities from a cycle race around the pickle fields to pickle tossing, pickle juice cocktails and a rather obscure gallery of pickle art.

📅 End of Apr
ℹ North Carolina Pickle Fest www.ncpicklefest.org
    North Carolina Tourism www.visitnc.com

28 Malecón | SOUTH AMERICA

Havana, Cuba

In the wet season, feisty waves can engulf Havana's resplendent Malecón (seawall promenade) but in the dry heat of summer the only deluge is the crowds. Synonymous with carefree family strolls, street theatre, jugglers, fishermen, cigar-puffing buskers and hand-holding couples, the Malecón is a focal point and gathering spot for Habaneros. Stretching 7 km (4 miles) from the colonial centre (Habana Vieja), this pulsing artery of the city was built in 1901 and has since housed public baths, car races, film

shoots, parades, domino players and concerts. Grand old buildings and statues overlook the passersby throwing offerings to the Yoruba gods into the blue-green depths of Havana Bay. Arrive just before the weather turns from dry to wet, mid-late April.

📅 Year-round, but weather turns from dry to wet in mid – late Apr
ℹ Cuba Tourism www.cubaldn.com

29 Chocolate Festival | EUROPE

Bruges, Belgium

Since the ancient Mayan civilizations, chocolate has been prized as a decadent indulgence, originally consumed in gooey liquid form and hailed as an aphrodisiacal boost. Among its many claims, chocolate is believed to produce a rapid heart rate, more intense than passionate kissing, when allowed to melt slowly in the mouth. Chocolate is also believed to be good for the skin (so long as it is slathered on rather than ingested). The aroma alone

is said to heighten sensitivity and euphoria and stimulate positive energy - thanks to the chemical Phenylethylamine (PEA), a constituent of chocolate that is also found in the brain and which increases as joy, pleasure and elation are experienced.

As the producer of 172,000 tons of chocolate each year and home to over 200 chocolate shops, Belgium is undisputed King of Chocolate – and a heaven for chocoholics. Renowned for high-grade sugar, creamy milk and rich cocoa, Bruges is drenched in the rich aroma of chocolate year-round. Hand-made Belgian chocolates are fresh, light, delicate and wholly preservative free with 100 per cent cocoa butter. Visitors can easily indulge in the pursuit of all-things chocolaty by sniffing out Bruges's sweetest attractions, be it tasting in at least a dozen forms or a tour of the city's chocolate history museum. Every plaza and backstreet hoasts an array of truffles, pralines and chocolate squares together with all manner of dark, milk and white chocolate treats. Bruges also hosts a sweet-smelling four-day Chocolate Festival "Choco-Laté" in spring each year – a date every sweet-toothed connoisseur should enter in their diary.

🗓 5 days, Apr - May

ⓘ Belgium Tourist Office www.visitbelgium.com
  Choco-Late www.choco-late.be

30 Fire Festival | EUROPE

Edinburgh, Scotland

Before the Romans divided the seasons into a calendar of 12 months, the Celtic year was marked by four Quarter Days: Beltane, Lughnasadh ('Luna-sa'), Samhuinn ('Sa-wain') and Imbolc. Each season was a time of great celebration with Beltane the biggest of the four festivities as the upcoming arrival of spring is heralded.

Today, the Beltane Fire Society throws an elaborate fire-and-costume festival that evokes the mystic rites of ancient Britons around Edinburgh's Carlton Hill. Drummers, dancers and a lurid assortment of elves, pagan devils, sprites and goddesses make-up a fire-lit procession led by the May Queen and her white-clad female warriors. Passing from the Castle Esplanade to Parliament Square in a cacophony of drums, bonfires and fire sculptures, the Fire Festival's exuberant partially-clothed, body-painted revellers breathe fire amidst the Beltane drummers as they belt out rhythms to usher in the spring.

🗓 Apr 30th

ⓘ Beltane Fire Festival www.beltane.org
  Edinburgh Tourism www.edinburgh.org

Mystic rites are celebrated in fire rituals and torch-led processions

May

1 Maypole Dancing

Since 1894, a garlanded pole has been woven with floral ribbons

Ickwell, England

Maypole Dancing has celebrated the onset of May for generations - in the Bedfordshire village of Ickwell records date from the 1560s and May Day festivities have taken place virtually there uninterrupted since 1894. On May Day, trees were cut down and stuck into the ground in the centre of the village. Villagers danced around the tree poles in celebration of the end of winter and the start of fine planting weather. Today, a May Queen is crowned after a floral procession and her flower-bearing attendants dance in colourful swirls of flowing petticoats around a garlanded pole on the village green weaving the ribbons in elaborate plaits in what is thought to be a pagan fertility ceremony.

📅 May Day Weekend

ℹ Ickwell May Day www.northill-parish.info/mayday

2 Lotus Lantern Festival

Seoul, Korea

In early May each year, in accordance with the lunar calendar, Koreans commemorate the birth of Buddha with a spectacular lantern festival (Yeondeung) in Seoul. First staged in AD866, the festival draws Buddhist devotees and general public alike. A symbolic lantern is placed in front of Seoul City Hall in honour of Buddha's birth. Snaking a route to Jogyesa Temple, a resplendent procession transforms the streets into a riot of colour with hand-held lotus-shaped lanterns and lantern floats in the shape of elephants, dragons and lotuses crafted from richly-coloured paper and silk. All day performances of traditional percussion music, dance, street theatre and acrobatics excite the crowds. As a finale, spectators join hands to perform a circular dance as 100,000 wish-lanterns are released into the clouds.

📅 3 days, early May

ℹ South Korea Tourism english.visitkorea.or.kr

3 Kentucky Derby

Louisville, Kentucky, USA

For over 130 years, this Grade I stakes race for three year-old thoroughbreds has been an annual fixture in Louisville, attracting America's premier jockeys, trainers and horse owners together with racing fans from all over the globe. The Derby, on the first Saturday in May, marks the end of a two-week horse-riding festival with a 2 km (1 mile) sprint at Churchill Downs. As a major centre of horse-breeding since the late 18th century, Kentucky is a natural venue for what has become known as the "most exciting two minutes in sport".

Aristides was the first winner of what is now called the Kentucky Derby, running the race in 2:37.75 over a mile and a half course. The fastest Derby was in 1973, by Secretariat, who broke the two-minute mark. Not only do horses average a weight loss of between 7 - 11 kg (15 - 25 lb) during a race but some wear out new shoes. Louisville boasts a number of Kentucky Derby traditions and customs with Mint Julep (a cocktail of bourbon, mint and sugar) the race's beverage of choice. Several hundreds of servings of thick stew of beef, chicken, pork and vegetables (called Burgoo) are sold each year.

📅 First Saturday in May

ℹ️ Kentucky Derby www.kentuckyderby.com
Kentucky Tourism www.kentuckytourism.com

A fiercely-fought 2 km (1 mile) sprint at Churchill Downs, known as the "most exciting two minutes in sport"

4 Antelope-hunting Festival | AFRICA

Winneba, Ghana

Winneba's centuries-old Aboakyer (Antelope Chasing Festival) is a calendar highlight in Ghana. Wearing full tribal regalia, two highly-primed opposing teams of Efutu warriors set off in hot pursuit of a fleeing bushbuck. Catching the beast alive, using nothing but bare hands, is the object of the contest – a test that separates the men from the boys. On capture, the antelope is carried to the tribal chief (Omanhene) who accepts it by stepping on it three times – before formally announcing its next-day slaughter to appease the fetish war god, Apa Sekum. The warriors – winners and losers – unite in the ritual, together with the whole community, enjoying many hours of feasting, dancing, beauty pageants and tribal celebrations amidst vari-coloured flags.

📅 Early May
ℹ Ghana Tourism www.touringghana.com

5 Friendship Festival | AFRICA

Marrakesh, Morocco

Around a quarter of a million Moroccans and Americans gather in an open sandy field for the Friendship Fest each May, just outside the stone walls of ancient Marrakech in Bab Ighli. Launched to celebrate friendship and peace between the two vastly different cultures, the event is hailed as a testament to religious tolerance and mutual respect. Over three nights, a diverse array of artists from both countries brings a festival of music to the city together with messages of unification and global peace. Each year's line-up covers a broad spectrum of contemporary and traditional Christian and Islamic artists in English, French and Arabic, from American gospel rock and acoustic folk to Pan-Islamic classics and traditional Moroccan beats.

📅 3 days, early May
ℹ Friendship Fest www.friendshipfest.com

Moroccan and American music talents combine

6 Processione Dei Serpari | EUROPE

A lively celebration of all things snake-like

Cocullo, Italy

Got a snake phobia? Then give the Feast Day of San Domenico in Cocullo a miss – unless confronting your fears is part of your therapy. On the first Thursday in May, hundreds of snakes are caught in the woods and carried back in sacks to the charming white-stone village, transforming its streets into a writhing mass of snakes. The Serpari (a clan of snake handlers unique to Cocullo) remove the fangs and drape the snakes around their necks while a feast celebrates this event with snake-shaped sweets, biscuits and breads.

📅 First Thursday in May

ℹ️ Italian Tourist Board www.italiantouristboard.co.uk

7 Canadian Tulip Festival | NORTH AMERICA

Ottawa, Canada

That the world's largest tulip festival isn't staged in Holland but Ottawa is something of a surprise. Canada's links with the Netherlands' favourite flower date back to 1946 when Princess Juliana bestowed 100,000 tulip bulbs in recognition of the city's role in liberating the Netherlands during WWII. This floral gesture sparked Ottawa's love affair with the bulbous Liliaceae and today, the tulip is a symbol of peace, freedom and friendship. In 1953, Canada's inaugural tulip festival showcased a few thousand plants. Within a decade this had grown to over two-million blooms of every species, sub-species, size and colour. Each May, more than 600,000 visitors visit the three-week event, prompting Ottawa to declare itself the Tulip Capital of North America – if not the world.

Over 2 million blooms attract more than 600,000 visitors

📅 18 days, May

ℹ️ Tulip Festival www.tulipfestival.ca

8 Celebrate the Coffee Harvest | SOUTH AMERICA

Chanchamayo Valley, Peru

Tufted coffee bushes clad every slope of the Chanchamayo Valley in the High Andres, a fertile emerald terrain that boasts a reputation for the finest coffee in Peru. Cultivating shade-grown quality Arabica beans, the Peruvian coffee capital is renowned for its mild acidity and produces crops of fulsome flavour tended by over 80,000 growers. Visit during May to September as ripe cherries are painstakingly picked for traditional micro-wet-milling. After processing their coffee, most farmers hike their beans by foot or mule into the nearest town – a trip that can take anywhere from 30 minutes to eight hours. On Saturdays, the town plazas become a frenzied market for the surrounding growers – the source of most of Peru's 5.9 million bags. Harvest celebrations in the Chanchamayo Valley are lively and long-lasting with hard-drinking and dancing in the region's many tiny mountain pueblos.

📅 May – Jun

ℹ Peru Tourist Board www.peru.info

Ripe cherries are painstakingly picked by hand by over 80,000 coffee growers

9 St Lucia Jazz Festival | NORTH AMERICA

St Lucia

It's hard to imagine that the St Lucia Jazz Festival was simply conceived to fill a gap in the island's off-season tourist calendar. Today, what started as a marketing ploy is a fully-fledged high-tempo St Lucian tradition that offers main stage big name artists from the Caribbean across all jazz genres, including acoustic, new age, fusion, R&B and Latin-American, together with fringe performances (such as poetry, art, dance and comedy), craft markets, food stalls and events.

📅 2nd – 10th May

ℹ St Lucia Jazz Festival stluciajazz.org

10 Geyser Eruptions

Yellowstone National Park, USA

An estimated 10,000 thermal features are part of Yellowstone Park's gurgling terrain – be it gushing geysers, steaming pools, hissing fumaroles, bubbling mud pots or warm seeps. Six mighty geysers send water exploding over 30 m (100 ft) on a daily basis while others simply splutter and splash. The most famous is Old Faithful, a forceful geyser that erupts every 45 to 90 minutes. Geologists believe underground magma sits just 64 km (40 miles) below the surface of the Earth's crust in Yellowstone – hence the abundance of superheated water. Hot pools radiate a rainbow of colours, depending on the intensity of light. Visit in the quietude of May for the brightest hues of spring.

Spring (quiet and bursting with colour)

Yellowstone National Park www.nps.gov/yell

Six mighty geysers spew superheated water skywards amidst steaming fumaroles and bubbling pools

11 Moose-spotting Along Moose Alley | NORTH AMERICA

New Hampshire, USA

The stretch of Route 3 that runs from Pittsburg, New Hampshire to the Canadian border isn't called Moose Alley without good reason – as around 10,000 resident moose will testify. Highway signs warn "Brake for Moose" as these mighty 550 kg (1,200 lb)-pound beasts have little regard for the rules of the road and can prove a formidable obsticle for speeding cars. Spring is an optimum time for moose encounters – they can often be seen licking the remains of roadside winter salt. The best times of the day are early morning and dusk as the animals tend to hide in the woods during the day. If you are unlucky enough not to meet a moose, the drive through some of the most beautiful landscape in the United States is still worth the trip.

📅 May

ⓘ New Hampshire Tourism www.visitnh.gov

'Moose Alley' is home to 10,000 beasts, many weighing over 550 kg (1,210 lb)

12 Prague Spring Festival | EUROPE

Czech Republic

First staged in 1946, Prague's Spring Festival has survived the twists and turns of history led by the century-old Czech Philharmonic. Today, it continues to garner the support of top soloists and orchestras and regularly debuts Prague's most phenomenal musical talent. As a founding member of the World Federation of International Musical Competitions, the Spring Festival commemorates individuals who have shaped the world of music.

📅 May 12th

ⓘ Prague Spring Festival www.festival.cz

13 Rose Festival | AFRICA

Kelaa, Morocco

The town of Kelaa M'Gouna is set amidst red cliffs, fields of fragrant Persian roses and castles in the Morocco's Valley of the Roses. Renowned for its fragrant rose oil and rose water, the region celebrates the annual flower harvest with a Rose Festival: a magical event characterized by folkloric displays, singing and handicrafts. During the festival, a Rose Queen is crowned to reign over the procession of floats decked with velvety blooms.

📅 3 days, mid May

ℹ Morocco National Tourist Office www.visitmorocco.com

Fragrant blooms and scented oils ensure Kelaa is sweet-smelling in May

14 Catwalks Over the Iguazú Falls | SOUTH AMERICA

A succession of tumbling cascades that form a foaming cauldren

Brazil-Argentina

Some 275 tumultuous waterfalls tumble over the cliffs at the border of Argentina and Brazil to form a foaming cauldron below a series of terrifying precipices - a convergence point dubbed the Devil's Throat Gorge. It is said that Argentina provides the show and Brazil enjoys the view of the Iguaza Falls – and is true that the cascades are best viewed from the Brazilian panoramic catwalks. These magnificent vantage points are reached via paths that snake through jungle rich in butterfly and bird life. Visit in spring when the mist and foam cause an almost permanent rainbow adding extra magic to the jaw-dropping views.

📅 For glorious rainbows and colours, the dry season Apr – end Jul. For full might, go when it's wet, Dec – Feb

ℹ Mexico Tourism www.visitmexico.com
   Argentine Department of Tourism www.turismo.gov.ar

15 Candle Race | EUROPE

Italy

Gubbio's Candle Race (Festa dei Ceri) provides a first-rate excuse to don elaborate historical costume in order to share in the spirit of one of Italy's liveliest medieval romps. A 900-year-old relay, involving 400 kg (885 lb) wooden columns rather than batons, draws crowds to the Piazza della Signoria. Representing a patron saint, each 'candle' is wetted with water on the stroke of midday and blessed. At 6pm, the race begins sending Ceraioli (candle bearers) charging off to the Basilica di Santa Ubaldo to delighted cheers.

📅 May 15th
ℹ Italian Tourist Board www.italiantouristboard.co.uk

16 Hike Mount Mulanje | AFRICA

Malawi

Rising up like a giant 650 sq km (250 sq mile) granite shield, the peaks of Mount Mulanje stand guard over southern Malawi's forested wilderness and grassy meadows. Jagged granite crags topple into lush valleys where waterfalls tumble into deep, cool swimming holes. Of the 20 peaks that exceed 2500 m (8,200 ft) Sapitwa marks the highest point in Central Africa (3000 m (9,840 ft)) providing a dry-season challenge (May to July) to walkers, guides and porters along narrow, steep mountain paths.

📅 late May – end of Jul
ℹ Overlanding Africa www.overlandingafrica.com
   Malawi Tourism www.malawitourism.com

17 Cannes Film Festival | EUROPE

France

One of the most prestigious events in the European calendar, the Cannes International Film Festival has captured the imagination of celebrity-watchers across the world for over six decades. Held annually (usually in May) at the glamorous Palais des Festivals et des Congres, the festival is as famous for its star-studded parties as its movie premieres. Numerous artsy hangouts fill with avid filmgoers and cinéphiles with lots of star-gazing opportunities when actors, producers, directors, VIPs and their entourages take to the Red Carpet processions four times a day.

📅 9 days, mid May
ℹ Festival de Cannes www.festival-cannes.com

18 Grizzly Bear Watching

Selkirk's old-growth rainforests are rich in nuts, berries and bears

Selkirk Mountains, Canada

Grizzly bears enjoy the freedom of thousands of acres of old growth rainforest in the Selkirk Mountains, foraging for berries and nuts. Beginning abruptly in Northern Idaho, the Selkirk boasts a striking series of peaks in British Columbia where both grizzlies and black bears can be spotted in secluded spots. Log cabins sit amidst unspoilt forests rich in moose, deer, coyote, elk, porcupine and grey wolf. For vibrant colour and re-awakening bears, visit May to June when lake flora is in full bloom.

- May – Jun (mountains are in full bloom)
- Grizzly Bear Ranch www.grizzlybearranch.ca
  Canada Tourism www.canada.travel

19 Ancient Yogyakarta

Java, Indonesia

Often described as Indonesia in miniature, Yogyakarta sits within the cradle of several Javanese empires surrounded by jungles, rice fields and mountain peaks. To stroll the old quarter of Yogyakarta (Kota Gede), is to delve into bustling markets filled with fine arts created by local craftsmen and painters. The Sultan's Palace (the Kraton) is a city within a city with opulent rooms lavishly appointed with gilded artwork and richly woven textiles. In the outer reaches of Yogyakarta, the countryside is home to picturesque temples and shrines bordered by the Indian Ocean and a string of volcanoes. Visit in May when rainfall is at its lowest and the skies are bright and clear.

- May (rainfall is at its lowest and the skies are bright and clear)
- YogYes Tourism www.yogyes.com
  Jogja Tourism www.jogjatourism.com

Ancient temples, shrines and markets characterise olden Yogkakarta

20 Bedouin Spice Therapies

Hajar Mountains, United Arab Emirates

In May, the desert hinterland in the foothills of the Hajar Mountains is arguably at its most scenic in a conservation zone that has successfully reintroduced the native Arabian Oryx. The Al Maha Desert Resort & Spa enjoys the tranquillity of an isolated setting just a 45 minute drive from the gridlocked traffic of fast-paced Dubai. Drawing on traditional Bedouin influences, the resort's individually styled suites echo conventional Arabic architecture and feature modern day comforts along with unique artwork, antiquities, hand-crafted furniture and Persian rugs. Soft music and golden sunsets heighten the romance of the desert. Al Maha's traditional Bedouin encampment is set amongst palms with unrestricted views across

the sands. Choose from a range of Persian-inspired therapies including an hour-long Desert Aroma Massage, a 90 minute Desert Hot Stone Massage and a grainy Desert Sand-Herb Rasoul scrub. Using pungent Arabian oils and traditional spices to leave skin silky-smooth and glowing, the Al Maha's touch-therapies reflect the timeless unhurried pace of the desert environs. The surrounding 225 sq km (87 sq mile) Dubai Desert Conservation Reserve allows guests to delve into indigenous cultures, spot wildlife and explore desert habitat.

📅 Year-round, but wildlife is more easily spotted in Spring

ℹ Al Maha Resort www.al-maha.com

Pungent Arabic spices, oils and desert sand are used in soaks, lotions and scrubs

21 Hebridean Cruise | EUROPE

Scotland

Stretching for 210 km (130 miles), the 200 islands of the Outer Hebrides run from north to south off the north-western coast of Scotland. A striking mix of terrain characterizes the archipelago, from wave lapped golden sand and bird-filled marshes to gusty heather-clad peaks. Only a handful of isles are inhabited, each with its own distinctive traditions and heritage. Salmon and trout loch fishing and sea angling are popular pursuits. Cruises aboard the *Hebridean Princess* set sail from Oban March to November (with May-June the nicest months weather-wise) to visit crofting communities, fishing harbours, otter colonies, seal-filled bays and the moorlands of Barra, Eriskay, Benbecula, Harris, Lewis and the remote island of St Kilda.

📅 Mar – Nov (with May – Jun the nicest months weather-wise)
ℹ️ Hebbridean Cruises www.hebridean.co.uk
 Hebrides Tourism www.visithebrides.com
 Visit Scotland www.visitscotland.org

22 Amazing Souks | ASIA

Sana'a, Yemen

Set on a 2,100 m (7,000 ft) plateau northeast of the port of Al Hudaydah amidst abundant fruit trees, the city of Sana'a boasts a resplendent old quarter with domed mosques, crumbling walls and cobblestone alleys. People spill onto the streets between after dark to eat, drink and haggle at the ramshackle collection of bazaars. Rich in jewellery, silver, silks and leather goods the Souk al-Milh is home to dimly-lit workshops where vibrant carpets are woven and sold. Stroll around sacks of spices, vegetables, pottery and copper cauldrons on a backdrop of beautifully preserved 400-year-old dark basalt stone.

📅 Spring, when temperatures are bearable
ℹ️ Yemen Tourist Board www.yementourism.com

Haggle amongst a labyrinth of ramshackle cobblestone alleyways

23 Urban Abseilling

Rotterdam, Holland

Abseiling Rotterdam's sleek, needle-thin Euromast tower presents a unique array of metropolitan hazards amidst steam-spewing vents and dive-bombing pigeons. High above the blaring horns of gridlocked streets a death-defying 100 m (328 ft) drop below, the tower offers a stomach-lurching plummet and a vertigo-inducing panorama – runs May to September, with 30 km (18 mile) views out to Belgium on a clear day.

23 May – Sep (with gorgeous views on a clear, spring day)

❶ Euromast www.euromast.nl

Rotterdam Tourism www.rotterdam.info

Brace yourself for a stomach-lurching 100 metre (328 ft) drop

24 Circuit of Mt Kailas

This towering snow-capped black rock is Tibet's most sacred site

Tibet

As the world's most venerated holy site, Mount Kailash is also the least visited. Soaring to over 22,000 ft in a remote corner of Tibet, it is considered a supremely sacred location by billions of people practising four religions. Mount Kailash has been revered since before the dawn of Hinduism, Buddhism and Jainism yet is seen by only a few thousand pilgrims each year. No planes, trains or buses journey anywhere near this towering snow-capped black rock - and overland driving is tough and unpredictable. For Tibetans, pilgrimage (neykhor) means "to circle around a sacred place" – and a 52 km (32 mile) circuit of Mount Kailash is doable in around 12 hours, from early May to August.

23 Early May – Aug

❶ Mount Kailash Guide www.snowjewel.com

25 Sport Fishing

Puerta Vallarta, Mexico

Water temperatures in outer Puerto Vallarta reach 28°C (83°F) May to October, bringing yellowfin tuna close to 180 kg (400 lb) within reach of this 19th-century fishing port. Yellowfin frequent depths of 100 fathoms and are distinctive for their silvery blue-black backs and broad yellow eye-to-tail stripe. The off-shore rocks of Roca Corbetena boast a shallow reef teeming with trophy-size glamour fish, including 3 m (9 ft) yellowfin - a challenge for even the saltiest sea-dog to land. Dozens of fishing charters ply for trade during Yellowfin season, from full-day to five-day trips on the Bahia de Banderas and the fish-rich waters of the Pacific Ocean.

🗓 May – Oct (yellowfin season)

ℹ Puerto Vallarta Tourism www.visitpuertovallarta.com

26 Zamberlan Adventure Trophy

Wisla, Poland

In May each year, the gruelling three-day Zamberlan Adventure Trophy brings the mad, bad and dangerous to Wisla, a small town on the border with the Czech Republic. Set in the ski-run riddled Silesian Beskids Mountains at the 1047 km (650 mile) Wisla River's source, the town is surrounded by woods, gorges and waterfalls. Umpteen well-marked paths run through the city and around it along relatively flat mountain ridges. Poland's most demanding physical challenge is a multi-disciplined event that combines MTB (mountain biking), trekking, trail-running, rope-work, zip-wiring, river kayaking and in-line skating .

Entrants arrive in Wisla for a kit inspection at noon on the Wednesday ahead of the Thursday morning start. Teams enter male-only, mixed and veteran categories in either the master class or amateur class – the latter is shorter at 225 km (140 mile) and is for mixed teams. The 350 km (217 mile) course includes 220 km (137 miles) of MTB, 95 km (59 miles) of trekking, 25 km (15 miles) of mountain river kayaking (two hours) and 20 km (12 miles) of in-line skating. All teams start simultaneously on a route marked by check points with competitors working with a tourist scale map –

Poland's most demanding physical challenge

team members are checked off but with freedom to determine the exact route. Teams must complete each check point formality and perform all special tasks - and must not exceed the time limit.

🗓 Weekend, May

ℹ Zamberlan Adventure Trophy www.adventuretrophy.pl
   Wisla Tourist Board www.wisla.pl

27 Cheese-rolling

Gloucestershire, England

Nobody seems able to ascertain the precise origins of Gloucestershire's ancient cheese-rolling contest. Or, what motivates a hundred competitors from as far afield as Japan, Australia and the US to hurtle down a treacherous slope in pursuit of a run-away cheese. What is certain, however, is that cheese-rolling at Cooper's Hill has taken place for centuries – initially as a Midsummer event and now as a celebration of spring. A guest roller starts the race by releasing a 3 kg (7-8 lb) round of cheese 200 m (656 ft) down a steep hillside. In hot pursuit, competitors chase the cheese in a reckless, running tumble. Brisk winds and torrential rain often add extra peril. The first person to arrive at the foot of the hill wins the cheese. The action starts at midday and lasts for around three hours.

🗓 Spring Bank Holiday

ℹ Cheese Rolling Contest www.cheese-rolling.co.uk

Cheese-rolling is a rambunctious, reckless and ruthless 3 hour pursuit

28 Mountain Biking in Moab

Utah, USA

Home to some of the greatest mountain biking on the planet, Moab boasts a host of scenic trails through canyons and mesa tops with the 16 km (10 mile) Slickrock Bike Trail the ultimate challenge. Winter is too cold to fully enjoy Moab's highlight: even riders who enjoy extremes wait for chill to pass. Set between Moab Valley and the Colorado River, the trail was established in 1969 for motorcycle riding and constantly changes elevation as it crosses a series of Navajo sandstone domes and fins. Steep ascents lead to narrow ledges and death-defying drop-offs. Allow around five hours to complete – longer if you're easily distracted by the colourful rock formations.

🗓 Spring (Apr – May)

ℹ Moab Tourism www.discovermoab.com

   Moab Cyclery www.moabcyclery.com

   Rim Cycle Tours www.rimtours.com

29 Travel on the Karakoram Highway | ASIA

Pakistan-China

The highest paved international road in the world, the spectacular Karakoram Highway stretches over 1,300 km (807 miles) to link Pakistan and China across the rugged Karakoram Mountains at 4,693 m (15,396 ft) through the long, flat Khunjerab Pass. A 20-year collaborative project by the Pakistani and Chinese governments, the Karakoram Highway was completed in 1986 and follows the fabled Silk Road. Closed in winter, and deluged by monsoons in summer, the weather is at is most predictable during spring and early autumn – but conditions can deteriorate rapidly even so.

📅 Spring and early Autumn
ⓘ Pakistan Tourist Office www.tourism.gov.pk
China National Tourist Office www.cnto.org

30 Trekking in the Kingdom of Mustang | ASIA

Nepal

Long isolated from the outside world, the Kingdom of Mustang has remained unchanged for centuries, to preserve some of the last vestiges of traditional Tibetan Buddhist culture. Located to the north of the mountain giants of Dhaulagiri and Annapurna, the Kingdom of Mustang is north of the main Himalayan range and geographically part of the highlands of Tibet. Trails are open to a few select trekking groups each season and wriggle through white-washed villages on an ancient trade route set amid barley fields, Buddhist monasteries, deep ravines and rocky ledges.

📅 Apr - May
ⓘ Safe Journeys www.safejourneys.co.uk
Nepal Trekking Info www.nepaltrekkinginfo.com

31 Summer Glacier Skiing | EUROPE

Zermat, Switzerland

Climb aboard a yellow-green electric bus and a cable car to journey from Zermatt to the Matterhorn glacier – at 3,883 m (12,739 ft) above sea level, Europe's highest sightseeing spot. Snow-cover is a 365-day-a-year phenomenon at the Matterhorn glacier offering a rare opportunity for Europe's summer skiers to head to the piste on home soil. What's more, the 360° panoramic views take in the Swiss, Italian and French Alps – a total of 38 spectacular 4,000-m (13,000-ft) peaks.

📅 A rare spot for summer skiing in Europe
ⓘ Zermatt Tourism www.zermatt.ch
Switzerland Tourism www.myswitzerland.com

Arctic Musk Ox Safari | EUROPE

Dovrefjell National Park, Norway

Norway's Arctic musk ox is a shy, unkempt bovine goliath that weighs in at half-a-tonne. From June to late August each year, dedicated safaris head into the bleak, treeless wilderness north of Lillehammer, just one of the four regions in the world in which the beast is found. Spotting these oddball masses of pungent, shaggy hair requires diligence – a gland on their forelock emits a secretion that ensures they are smelt before they are sighted. Norwegian ox safaris are quite unlike the African-style jeep safaris that transport you to within a few metres of the creature in comfort – almost all the expedition takes place on foot. Long, uphill treks lead from one remote wooden hut to another to the so-called Roof of Norway in notoriously unpredictable weather conditions. Musk ox is known to inhabit Dovrefjell National Park, a 1,693 sq km (654 sq mile) glacier-sculpted moss-shrouded expanse where plant life predates the last ice age. At about 1.5 m (5 ft) tall, the musk ox can be dangerous with long, curled horns that jut from a mat of woolly hair. They can reach speeds of about 30 kph (17 mph) when agitated – much faster than the average human.

📅 Jun – late Aug

ℹ️ Musk Oz Safari Company www.moskussafari.no
Norway Tourist Bureau www.visitnorway.com

 Afro-Colombian Cooking | SOUTH AMERICA

Isla San Andres, Colombia

Lucy Trigidia Chow Robinson, known throughout the palm-scattered San Andres archipelago as 'Lucy in the Sky with Diamonds', delights visitors with her culinary traditions, wisdom and wit. Dressed in gold-and-tangerine robes this larger-than life 'Island Girl' adores her native food, cooking up a storm in a rustic kitchen – and allowing visitors the opportunity to experience the island's Afro-Colombian cuisine. Savour rondón (a slow-cooked stew of conch, yucca, plantain and dumpling cooked with coconut milk); the island's sweet-fleshed crab; fried fish and baked po (a traditional roasted pork) together with mango pies, Johnny cake and coconut bread. Visit during Independence celebrations in June to wash it down with the region's home-distilled rum ('bushy') – a potent brew that has survived piracy, war, slavery, immigration, sugar, cotton and religion.

📅 Year-round, though Jun is perfect as the islands are quiet and crowd-free

ℹ️ Lucy Trigidia Chow Robinson Tel: 513 2233;
Cell: 311 808 9039, email: lucytrigidia@yahoo.com
Travel the Unkown www.traveltheunknown.com

3 The Dreaming

Northern Territory, Australia

Several thousand culture-vultures head to the Northern Territory for its vibrant annual showcase of some of the most exciting, thought-provoking and disturbing Indigenous arts. Over four days, audiences at The Dreaming descend on an array of atmospheric venues (from sacred grounds and open-air stages to camp fires) to listen to tribal elders, musicians and comedians at workshops, shows and seminars. Installation art features vast works in stone, bone, wood and shell. Sunset soirées provide an opportunity to mingle with musicians, film-makers, songwriters, poets, dramatists, pseudo academics and authors inspired by dreamtime in events that explore storytelling, drumming circles, didgeridoo, ancient ceremonial rituals and rock paintings.

📅 4 days, early Jun

ℹ️ The Dreaming Festival www.thedreamingfestival.com

4 Night Diving in the Red Sea

Egypt

The vibrant underwater world of Egypt's Red Sea coast looks very different once the sun goes down and nocturnal marine life emerges from daytime nooks and crannies. Diving at night requires a period of adjustment so eyes become accustomed to the shadows and senses sharpen, guided by strobe-illuminated marker buoys and chemical light sticks. Crimsons, yellows and oranges in particular appear more intense against the darkness.

From Wadi Lahami over 20 different offshore dive sites can be reached. Dive into translucent depths rich in swim-throughs, tunnels, arches, caves and caverns. Octopi unravel in space-like slow-motion and groups of twinkling minute organisms add fairy-dust to the sea. Many species of crustaceans and molluscs use the night hours to feed – as do their predators – but it pays not to be overly-scared of what might be lurking beyond the dive light's beam. Just point it in an interesting looking area and take the time to examine it inch-by-inch whilst revelling in the increased activity on the reefs in the night-time glow.

Senses sharpen when diving at night and nocturnal marine life emerges

📅 Jun, when the reefs are less busy

ℹ️ Egyptian Tourist Board www.egypt.travel

5 Night Marathon | EUROPE

Venice, Italy

Around 4,000 participants limber up for Italy's Night Marathon along a stunning 42 km (26 mile) route that winds its way around beaches, lagoons and pine forests. The pretty resort of Cavallino Treporti, 15 km (9 miles) from Venice, denotes the start of this event. Athletes battle it out at pace, while fun-runners plod around bird-filled mud-flats. In the meantime a full-on party of 90,000 people rages from sunset to 6am at Cavallino's St Maria Elisabetta Square.

📅 Early Jun

ℹ️ Night Marathon www.nightmarathon.it

Over 4,000 runners compete overnight for the Night Marathon medal

6 Nashville Country Music Festival | NORTH AMERICA

USA

For country music lovers, there is only one place in the world to be each year in June. In this magic month, the home of country music plays host to its biggest party: a four-day celebration of all things country with 70 hours of live music involving over 400 hundred artists. Nashville has been inextricably linked with the sound of country since the early 1920's and the days of the Grand Ole Opry. Today every saloon bar, diner, dance hall and honky-tonk music club on Lower Broadway resonates with good old heel-kicking country refrains. Yet it is Nashville's Country Music Festival that truly lures the Stetson-and-jeans crowds. Over 145,000 country-lovin' dudes enjoy some of the world's greatest artists and upcoming talent at concerts, jamming sessions and free gigs .

📅 4 days in Jun

ℹ️ Country Music Festival www.cmafest.com
Nashville Tourism www.visitmusiccity.com

7 Jousting at Trakai Castle | EUROPE

Lithuania

In early June, Lithuania's Trakai Peninsula plays host to a weekend of Medieval-style pomp and pageantry during a jousting tournament that draws on the 11th century traditions of Sir Galahad and Sir Lancelot. In eras past, jousting helped keep armour-clad knights in prime condition during peace time pursuing chivalrous challenges for a lady's honour on thundering steeds. Today, at the Trakai Peninsula Castle Jousting Festival, teams of knights from all over the world compete on a rousing backdrop of bridges, towers and battlements. Step across a vast wooden drawbridge to enter Lithuania's symbol of sovereignty and power amidst shields and armour, bows and arrows, maces, stables and squires.

📅 Weekend, early Jun
ℹ Lithuania Tourist Board www.lithuaniatourism.co.uk
   Trakai Castle www.trakai.info

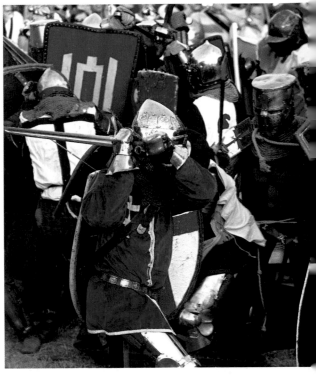

Expect plenty of medieval-style pomp and pageantry

8 Lavender Festival | NORTH AMERICA

Oregon, USA

For centuries, the lavender plant has been essential to herbal medicine in oils, seed form and crushed flowers. Believed to have curative benefits, lavender has antiseptic and anti-inflammatory properties (during WWI it was used as a disinfectant). A single drop of extract in a bathtub not only adds perfume but also calms, soothes and heals while a droplet of oil aids restful sleep. These therapeutic properties add a blissfull tranquility to the annual Oregon Lavender Festival in June where lavender is celebrated in all its glory, in bouquets, pomanders, sachets, essential oils and scented candles.

📅 Jun
ℹ Oregon Lavender Festival www.oregonlavenderfestival.org
   Oregon Tourism www.traveloregon.com

9 Freestyle Kayaking

Lyon, France

To the French it is La Feysinne, to the rest of the world it is "Hawaii sur Rhône"; a huge, perilous, crested wave that provides one of the most exciting urban freestyle kayaking venues on the planet. River Rhône's natural standing wave and tidal surges attract paddlers from all around the world in May and June to do battle with the Rhône's unpredictable forces. The Hawaii sur Rhône hosts the Lyon River Festival, a thrilling extreme-sport challenge that attracts top-flight paddling champions to France in June each year. Open to both freestyle and 'big air' competitors the festival boasts a weekend-long programme of events. Yet it is Lyon's incredible two-channelled wave that steals the show, be it long, steep, fluffy, glassy or foamy it is always oh-so-loud it positively roars.

23 Jun

ⓘ Lyon Tourism Board www.en.lyon-france.com

Unpredictable standing waves and tidal surges on the Rhone River has created a buzz with kayakers across the world

10 Cable-car Bell Ringing Competition | NORTH AMERICA

San Francisco, USA

Clang, clang, clang went the trolley in May 1949 when the first San Francisco Cable Car Bell Ringing Contest was born in the city's famous Union Square. Signalling a bright, new era for San Francisco's cable car system, previously on the brink of closure, the contest became an annual fixture in 1955. Construction of the first stretch of cable track began on Clay Street in 1873. A monument erected in Victorian Park pays tribute to local woman Freidel Klussmann for her successful campaign to save the network. Numerous mechanical gizmos together with old photographs and vintage cable cars can be found at the historic Washington/Mason cable car barn. The contest takes place in the first or second week in July, drawing hundreds of cable car enthusiasts from across the city – and beyond.

📅 Jun

ℹ Cable Car Museum www.cablecarmuseum.org
San Francisco Tourism www.onlyinsanfrancisco.com

Honouring the trolley bell since 1955

11 Miaoulis Festival | EUROPE

Hydra, Greece

A bastion of olden traditions, Hydra's only transport is walking, donkey or boat. Set in the Argo-Saronic Sea, approximately 80 km (50 miles) south of Athens, Hydra's liveliest festival is a week-long affair dedicated to Admiral Miaoulis, a homespun hero born in 1769. During the Greek War of Independence, Miaoulis' military action helped overthrow the Turks.

Today, boat races, swimming contests, torch-lit parades and folk dances lead to a dramatic re-enactment of the burning of an Ottoman flagship – a patriot finale.

📅 7 days, Jun

ℹ Greek National Tourism Organisation www.gnto.gr

12 Feast of St Anthony

Lisbon, Portugal

Portugal's Feast of St Anthony is sardine heaven, a tradition born out of a miracle. Whilst St Anthony was delivering a sermon on the shoreline, some sardines raised their heads out of the water to listen - bringing him nationwide fame. Modern festivities begin with mass where bread-sellers hawk little, round bread rolls for pressing against a bronze bust or painted portrait of the saint. The tradition of 'St Anthony's Bread' goes back to AD1263 when a child drowned in the Brenta River in Padua. The distraught mother pledged a gift to the poor of bread equal to her son's weight should St Anthony bring the boy back to life. He did, and the tradition was born. Today, the saint is also renowned as a matchmaker and on the eve of June 13th, girls try various methods of finding out whom they will wed, such as filling their mouths with water and holding it until a boy's name is mentioned.

📅 12th – 14th Jun

ℹ️ Portugal Tourism   www.visitportugal.com

13 Calcio Fiorentino (Medieval Football)

Florence, Italy

Though the rules were written in 1580, Calcio Fiorentino had already been played for centuries by teams of muscular, tattooed men stripped to the waist. History's most famous match took place in 1530 whilst Florence was under siege by the Spanish army. A game of Calcio provided the ultimate two-fingered gesture to a hostile enemy with the entire match played in full view of advancing troops. The game had died out by 1739, but was resurrected by Benito Mussolini in the 1930s. Today the annual grudge match allows old scores to be settled on the Piazza Santa Croce during a highly-physical mix of soccer, rugby and martial arts that was once Italy's primary football game.

📅 Jun

ℹ️ Florence Tourism   www.firenzeturismo.it

14 Gnaoua Festival

Essaouira, Morocco

Now more than a decade old, Essaouira's Gnaoua Festival attracts over 500,000 music fans with a rich programme of exciting sub-Saharan hybrid sounds on ten individual stages. A global line-up draws from a melange of Korean, European and Caribbean artists so expect the maverick fusing of guembri and castanets with trumpet and saxophone together with electro-contemporary North-African beats.

📅 4 days, late Jun – early Jul

ℹ️ Gnaoua Festival   www.festival-gnaoua.co.ma
  Morocco National Tourist Office   www.visitmorocco.com

Over 50,000 music fans descend on Essaouira for the sub-Saharan festival

15 Antarctic Midwinter Festival | AUSTRALIA/PACIFIC

Tasmania, Australia

Hobart's celebrated nine-day Antarctic Midwinter Festival pays homage to the winter solstice with a host of Antarctic-themed events such as polar walks, sledding, lantern parades, ice sculptures and bracing ice-water swims. Poetry, art, film, sporting challenges and parties highlight the heroic age of Antarctic exploration together with the beauty and wildlife of the region, and recreations of great husky races.

📅 9 days over Summer Solstice (Jun)
ℹ Tasmania Tourism www.discovertasmania.com

16 Midnight Swimming | EUROPE

Hämeenlinna, Finland

Finland's southern pine-covered headlands hug the placid waters of Lake Vanajavesi, where summer tourists spend lazy days soaking up warm rays on grassy knolls. Finns relish the summertime after the bitter cold of winter and gather around lakes and in green spaces in every waking hour. In June, an egg-yolk sun waits until after midnight to dip below the horizon after hours of slowly-unfolding crimson-pink hues. The locals swear this is the best time to bathe in Lake Vanajavesi when the barely dusk-like shimmer casts its silver shadows across the shore.

📅 Jun – Aug (Jun is quietest 'til Midsummer)
ℹ Finland Tourism www.visitfinland.com

17 Ancient Bushmen Rock Paintings | AFRICA

Tohlong, Lesotho

Blood-red etchings adorn a shelter just north of Tohlong on a site renowned as an ancient hunting spot. Using poisoned arrows, a Bushman would stalk his prey for several days, before finally going in for the kill. Detailed imagery depicts eland (one of the most spiritually potent creatures in bushman mythology) together with fat-bellied human and feline figures that symbolize malevolent forces and medicine men. In the clear, bright skies of the dry season, the muted hues of these three-dimensional rock paintings are at their best.

📅 May – Sep (Dry Season)
ℹ Lesotho Tourism www.lesotho.gov.ls

Tohlong's 3D rock paintings depict ancient mythology in muted hues

18 Blueberry Festival | NORTH AMERICA

Texas, USA

The oldest town in Texas, Nacogdoches' claim to fame is its plentiful crops of blueberries – an abundant harvest that is honoured in June in a party dubbed the "most delicious" in the state. On the city's main square, several tons of fresh blueberries are sold in every style imaginable, from pancakes, pies, muffins and cobblers to ice-cream sodas and wine. Blueberry farms open to festival-goers for tours and pick-your-own trips – a crowd-pulling pie-eating contest is a riot of pastry and blueberry cream.

📅 Mid Jun

ℹ️ Texas Blueberry Festival www.texasblueberryfestival.com
Texas Tourism www.traveltex.com

June's plentiful blueberry harvest has put Nacogdoches on the tourist map

19 White Nights

EUROPE

St Petersburg, Russia

During May to July, when the North Pole is tipped towards the sun, St Petersburg's sun never dips far beneath the horizon – even at night. The glow adds a poetic shimmer to a fairytale cityscape of glided domes and spires. Although White Nights are not unique to the city, St Petersburg enjoys this eternal twilight in a particularly romantic style. Forget madcap revelry, the common celebration is a stroll along the River Neva, to relish a night sky that is curiously, and beautifully, indistinguishable from day.

📅 Jun – Jul
ℹ Russia Tourism www.visitrussia.org.uk

Stroll along the River Neva to revel in the eternal glow of St. Petersburg's white nights

20 National Hollerin' Contest

NORTH AMERICA

North Carolina, USA

Every year, on the third Saturday in June, the otherwise sleepy hamlet of Spivey's Corner in North Carolina is transformed as 10,000 out-of-towners converge on a population of less than 100 people for the National Hollerin' Contest – a fixture since the summer of 1969. Established to revive the lost art of good old fashioned yelling, the first Spivey's Corner contest attracted crowds of entrants and spectators to the town. North Carolina's proud vocal tradition served as a means of long-distance communication between field workers and farmers before the introduction of the telephone. Since then, a number of esteemed guests have been invited to give public yelling a try, including former US president Ronald Reagan and the Shah of Iran. Today it's become a summer ritual for contestants from around the world with male-only, women and children's events for those prepared to convene clear their throat, and give it their all.

📅 Saturday mid Jun
ℹ National Hollerin Contest www.hollerincontest.com

21 Summer Solstice

Öland, Sweden

Even the Swedes themselves will readily admit to a strange, midsummer silliness – a symptom, they say, of being sensible and practical for the rest of the year. Together with Christmas, Midsummer (Midsommar) is the most popular festival in Scandinavia – a traditional celebration that pre-dates Christian times. Once a fertility ritual that centred on nature and the onset of the harvest season, the Summer solstice is time to gather friends and family together for fresh strawberries, smoked fish and pickled herring – washed down with plenty of beer. Many Swedes still decorate their houses inside and out with floral wreaths and bow-strewn birch garlands, while in rural Sweden, maidens dance around ribbon-swathed poles to ancient folk songs. In Öland, a small island on the Baltic Coast, giant bonfires are lit to ward off evil spirits and signify the defeat of darkness. Reached from Kalmar via a 6 km (4 mile) bridge, Öland is synonymous with wild Midsummer partying. In Stockholm, crowds of revellers drink beer and picnic by the capital's many lakes and waterways – in olden times, people would gaze into the depths to see the face of their future spouse. Today, the custom of the young is to simply jump in – naked.

🗓 21 – 23rd Jun
ℹ Swedish Tourism www.visitsweden.com
  Oland Tourism www.smaland-oland.com

Even the most sensible Swede resorts to a strange, summer silliness

22 Ladies Day

Ascot, England

Colloquially known as 'Ladies Day', the Gold Cup remains the feature race of the third day of Royal Ascot. Synonymous with posh frocks, smart suits and daring hats the Gold Cup switches the focus from horses to fashion. Queen Ann founded the Ascot Races in 1711 and it is still a royal sporting highlight.

23 Jun (busiest day of a 5 day Royal Ascot race meeting)

ⓘ Ascot Racecourse www.ascot.co.uk

Women dress up to the nines on Ladies Day, a tradition since 1711

23 Winter Solstice

Cairns, Australia

Queensland's colour-filled Winter Solstice Celebration combines rustic outback camping under canvas with music, dance and art in the Tablelands, a two-hour drive west of Cairns. Over 80 top DJs, bands and internationals artists entertain many thousands of festival-goers together with fire-dancers, workshops, market stalls, spiritual healing centres, funky kites and bushwalking treks.

23 21st – 23rd Jun (varies)

ⓘ Tropical Australia North Queensland www.tropicalaustralia.com.au

24 The Parade of the Pigs

Balayan, Batangas, Philippines

First a porker in a tutu, then a hog dressed as Snow White, before a pig in full ER scrubs and a toga-wearing swine. The Parada ng Lechon (Roasted Pig Parade) is no ordinary festival, with around 100 or so spit-roasted pigs in full fancy dress. Held annually on June 24th in the village of Balayan, the festival celebrates the feast day of St John the Baptist (San Juan), the region's patron saint. A mix of Catholic Christianity from the missionary teachings of the Spanish and the pagan rituals of the pre-Colonial peoples, the Roasted Pig Festival attracts thousands of tourists each year. Once dolled-up, the crispy-skinned pigs are paraded around the village on motorized floats – much to the delight of the salivating cheering crowds. Some snatch bite-sized chunks of meat as the parade passes by. Firecrackers fill the air as adults and children alike shoot each other with water pistols to evoke the purifying baptism of Jesus.

Each pig has been cooked over charcoal for at least five hours and basted with a brush made from leaves for extra succulence. Once dressed (according to the theme of the owner), the lechon is carried to the Church of Immaculate Conception for a special mass, after which it is blessed. Once the parade is over, all thoughts turn to the much-awaited consumption of the lechon as the partying and drinking begins.

📅 Jun 24th

ℹ Philippines Tourism www.tourism.gov.ph

A surreal parade of crispy-skinned pigs in fancy dress

25 Game of the Bridge | EUROPE

Pisa, Italy

Fiercely upheld, the tradition of the Gioco del Ponte (or Game of the Bridge) takes place on the last Sunday in June. With considerable pride at stake, 12 teams are pitted against each other in a series of battles, representing the opposing north and south banks of the River Arno: the bridge a symbol of the gulf between them. Dating back to 1568, the contest was fought using cudgels in one-to-one violent combat. A mighty battle between two teams (Mezzogiorno and Tramo) signalled the final day of fighting, this time between two teams. Each laid claim to half of the bridge, held by the opposing team. Whichever team seized power won the conquest. Today, only the team element remains in the Gioco del Ponte but proud displays of might are still at the core of the battles. Men pull a seven ton wagon over the Ponte di Mezzo, Pisa's old Roman bridge. Each team wears medieval garb, signifying the origins of the games.

Expect proud displays of power and might during Gioco del Ponte

📅 Last Sunday in Jun

ℹ Pisa Tourist Office www.pisaturismo.it

26 Safaricom Marathon | AFRICA

Kenya

There are few more extraordinary places on Earth to run a marathon than a Kenyan wildlife reserve – but entrants to the Safaricom Marathon do just that. Ranked amongst the 10 toughest marathon events, Safaricom's rough terrain and harsh climatic conditions entice long distance runners from all over the world. Located at an average altitude of 1676 m (5,500 ft) above sea level, runners not only have dizziness to contend with but also the threat of big game. Armed rangers, helicopters and spotter aircraft keep a permanent and watchful eye to ensure all 650 runners make the finish line - alive.

📅 Mid - late Jun
ℹ️ Sarfaricom www.lewa.org
     Kenya Tourism www.magicalkenya.com

27 Glastonbury Festival | EUROPE

Somerset, England

In September 1970, on the day after Jimi Hendrix died, the first Glastonbury Festival took place with Marc Bolan topping the bill. Entry cost £1 (including fresh milk from the farm) with an attendance of 1,500. In 1971, it moved to coincide with the Summer Solstice to become a festival "a la Woodstock" with the now-famous pyramid stage built along the Glastonbury–Stonehenge ley line. In the following decades, the festival underwent vast expansion with guest acts that included David Bowie, Van Morrison, Curtis Mayfield, Joe Cocker and the Velvet Underground alongside upcoming bands. By 2005 attendance had topped 150,000 with acts spanning all musical genres, from fringe rock, hip hop greats and R&B gurus to folk heroes and bastions of punk. Today's festival remains very much "a weekend of music, theatre, poetry in a field" – though it is now televised world-wide. However, the event still famously contends with the unpredictable British weather, though Glastonbury resiliently refuses to be a wash-out. In 1997 – the so-called 'Year of the Mud' – festival-goers partied undeterred to Sting, The Prodigy and Massive Attack wearing Wellington boots and 'war paint' of freshly-daubed sludge.

The UK's festival highlight à la Woodstock

📅 Last weekend in Jun
ℹ️ Glastonbury Festival www.glastonburyfestivals.co.uk
     Glastonbury Tourism www.glastonbury.co.uk

28 Sea-kayaking Greenland's Fjords | EUROPE

Greenland

As the birthplace of the Inuit qajaq, Greenland's coastal waters offer the expedition sea-kayaker some of the very finest paddling in the world – thousands of miles of unpopulated shoreline, shimmering waters, dramatic sunsets, creaking glaciers and jagged iceberg peaks offer innumerable intrepid adventures.

🗓 Summer (Jun – end of Aug)
ℹ Greenland Tourism www.greenland.com

Sea-kayaking Greenland's fjords offers blissful tranquility

29 Battle of the Wines | EUROPE

Rioja, Spain

Rioja's infamous Batalla de Vino in Haro is testament to what can happen when a land dispute gets out of hand. Every St Pedro's day since 1906 townsfolk have commemorated the 10th century wrangles over the Montes Obarenes with neighbouring town Miranda De Ebro in a mock fight. Dozens of family-run bodegas and vineyards open for Haro's wine-drenched folkloric party in which Rioja-stained revellers spray each other from wineskins (botas), jugs and containers whilst spectators shriek and swig away

🗓 Jun 29th
ℹ www.labatalladelvino.com

30 Queenstown Winter Festival | AUSTRALIA/PACIFIC

New Zealand

An eclectic array of diverse events are shoe-horned into the Queenstown Winter Festival – a 10-day frenzy of concerts, balls, competitions, races, fireworks, bands, comedy, debates, food and wine tasting. Festival organizers boast that the event is *so* jam-packed there's no room for even the skinniest of buskers. Now one of New Zealand's ultimate winter parties, Queenstown Winter Festival has been over 35 years in the making – after a group of drinkers in a pub decided the cold nights and snow were worth relishing with gusto. These days, the town heaves with around 60,000 fun-loving winter celebrants.

🗓 10 days, Jun – Jul
ℹ Winter Festival www.winterfestival.co.nz

July

1 Henley Royal Regatta

| EUROPE

Oxfordshire, England

Held annually ever since 1839, except during two world wars, Henley Royal Regatta is considered one of the finest competitive amateur rowing events by oarsmen all over the world. Originally an afternoon event, today's five-day regatta is a lavish affair as famous for its champagne tents, chic outfits and gourmet lunches as for its coxless fours, double sculls and eights. Thousands of people line the Thames to cheer on their favourite rowers.

📅 First week in Jul

ℹ Henley Festival www.henley-festival.co.uk

Much Champagne is quaffed during this lavish Thames-side rowing event

2 Fiesta de Santa Librada

| SOUTH AMERICA

Las Tablas, Panama

To sample almost every aspect of Panamanian culture in a single weekend, head to Las Tablas for the Santa Librada festival. Thousands of people from all over Latin America swamp this small town by early morning Friday. Most head straight for the *seco* tent (Panama's fiery liquor of fermented sugar cane) to get the party started before the bull-roping, sandal-making contests, dancing and fiercely-fought pollera (national dress) pageant begins.

📅 Early Jul, weekend

ℹ Panama Tourist Board www.visitpanama.com

3 Singapore Food Festival

| ASIA

Singapore

Singapore's fusion culture extends to its food traditions with a generous dollop of Malay, Chinese, Indian and European influence in each and every Singaporean dish. Flavours are robust, flavoursome and frequently spicy as Chinese condiments, Indian spices, Malay herbs (lemongrass, chillies, coconut and galangal) collide with European culinary techniques – as each ancestral lands brings its unique style of cooking to the Singaporean pot. Even the roadside food hawkers in this vibrant city-state boast a gourmet tradition – a style of fast-food unlike any other that is undoubtedly one of the more colourful characteristics of Singapore cuisine.

Food is at the heart of Singapore. Any time of day, or night, you'll find an endless variety of cuisine served hot or cold in this cosmopolitan and multicultural metropolis – especially during Singapore's week-long Food Festival in July. The event offers innumerable opportunities to savour the many colours, textures and flavours of the island. Follow your nose to Parco Bugis Junction where wooden tables and chairs under canvas represent a zillion food zones. Visit a sizzling array of aromatic food stalls to try laksa (rich and spicy coconut gravy served with rice noodle, prawns, fish cake and tau pok), Hainanese chicken rice (poached chicken and fragrant rice with chilli, ginger and black soy sauce), mee siam (rice vermicelli with prawns in tangy assam gravy), satay: juicy chunks of roasted marinated meat on skewers and chilli crab (prepared with a hearty sauce of fresh chillies, tomato sauce, fresh eggs and spring onions).

📅 1 month, from early Jul
ℹ️ Singapore Food Festival www.singaporefoodfestival.com
   Singapore Tourism www.visitsingapore.com

4 Fourth of July | NORTH AMERICA

East River, New York, USA

Some call it Independence Day, many simply "the fourth of July", or in the words of Founding Father John Adams, America's "great anniversary festival." In honour of the 1776 declaration, communities across America break out in a riot of stars-and-stripes pomp and tickertape pageantry at picnics, barbecues and street parties. For over three decades, Macy's department store has sponsored what it bills as the nation's largest July 4th firework party: a 30 minute show of 35,000 shells launched from barges on the East River and New York Harbour that draws 3 million people onto the streets. Tune into local station 1010 WINS for rousing classical music in perfect synch with the pyrotechnics. Arrive very early to grab a front-line spot on the river, the South Street Seaport or Brooklyn Heights Promenade.

📅 July 4th
ℹ️ New York State Tourism iloveny.com

35,000 fireworks entertain over 3.5 million New Yorkers

5 Wife-carrying Championships | EUROPE

Finland

The gold medal winner in Finland's World Wife-carrying Championship wins their wife's weight in beer. Rules dictate wives should be aged over 17 and weigh a minimum of 49 kg (108 lb). At 253.5 m (832 ft), the track runs from sand to grass and gravel with two obstacles to climb over, as well as a metre-deep stretch of water. Techniques vary, from the "Estonian Carry" (where the woman clamps her thighs to the sides of the man's face while hanging upside down on his back) to riding piggyback, sitting on the man's shoulders or being hauled fireman style. With its roots in stealing women the contest is staged in the remote village of Sonkajarvi, a few hours' drive from the Arctic Circle. Thousands of spectators cheer the competitors on - whooping when a wife is dropped and a 15-second penalty is incurred.

📅 First Saturday in Jul

ℹ️ Finland Tourism www.visitfinland.com

Women must weigh over 49 kg (108 lb) to be eligible for this oddball dash

6 Fijian Firewalking | AUSTRALIA/PACIFIC

Only the villagers of Bequa Island have fire-walking skills in Fiji

Beqa, Fiji

To ceremonial chants, tribesmen on the Fijian island of Beqa embark on the ritual of *vilavilairevo* (jumping into the oven) by stepping onto a pit of white-hot coals. Beqa's people are believed to have captured a spirit god (Tui Namoliwai) who promised supernatural powers over fire in exchange for release. Today, the nine villages on Beqa and their 200 residents begin firewalking as early as 8 am - a mindboggling spectacle that does the villagers no harm.

📅 10 days, Jul – Aug

ℹ️ Fiji Visitors Bureau www.fijime.com

7 Singing Sticks Festival | EUROPE

Northampton, England

Northamptonshire in the English Midlands may be a hell of a long way from the wilds of the Aussie outback but that doesn't prevent it from pulsating with the deep, throaty, melodic hums of several hundred didgeridoos at the Singing Sticks Festival every July. Set in a grassy field edged by woods, the festival attracts "didge" aficionados from far and wide to tented workshops, concerts, jamming sessions and chill out zones warmed by fire pits.

The didgeridoo is a musical instrument of the Aboriginal peoples of northern Australia, consisting of a long hollow branch or stick that makes a deep drone when blown into. The instrument is made from living Eucalyptus trees, which have had their interiors hollowed out by termites. At the Singing Sticks Festival there is a disctinctly laid-back and chilled-out vibe, with an emphasis on enjoying the music of the didgeridoo and honing your playing skills. The venue is set in a large area of open woodland, and camping facilities enable didgeridoo fanatics to stay on site.

📅 Mid – Jul

ℹ️ Singing Sticks Festival www.singingsticks.co.uk

8 Redneck Games | NORTH AMERICA

Georgia, USA

Georgia's Redneck Games in East Dublin every July are taken very seriously by the 10,000 rednecks that attend. Participants prepare year round for events like the mud-pit belly flop, bobbing for pig's feet, seed spitting, dumpster diving, bug zapping and the armpit serenade. Originally dubbed the Bubba-Olympics (as a spoof of the 1966 Olympics in Atlanta) the event was launched in 1995 by radio station WQZY as a publicity stunt and to stick two fingers up at America's politically-correct brigade. Today, the Redneck Games continues to belch in the face of its critics and is covered by newspapers and television stations all over the country - beer bellies and all.

📅 Saturday, early – mid-Jul

ℹ️ Summer Redneck Games
www.summerredneckgames.com

A contestant perfects the beer-belly-flop at the Redneck Games

9 Oil Wrestling

Turkey

Since the days of the Ottoman Empire, oil wrestling (Yağh Gűreş) has been Turkey's gutsy national sport, celebrated in a 650-year-old tournament in Kirkpinar near the ancient capital of Edirne. Turkish Oil Wrestling was championed by the Ottoman Sultan, Orhan Gazi and his elite fraternity of body guards who would wrestle every night around camp.

According to legend, a closely-fought match once continued all night and the following day, until both opponents died through sheer exhaustion. On returning to the burial site years later, the Sultan was astounded to see that forty springs had arisen where the bodies had been laid. He named the land Kirkpinar (40 springs) - and it has been the venue of the tournament ever since.

Prior to combat, the wrestlers slather themselves in oil from head to toe and put on the traditional garb of thick leather shorts (Kispet) made from water buffalo hide. Matches are won when the defeated opponent is held face upward towards the sky. For three days, a thousand barefoot grapplers do battle in simultaneous matches in eleven divisions, ranging from school age teens to veteran champions. The sun is hot and the fights are long with few forbidden holds and grabs. However, while this man-to-man combat can be fiercely aggressiveness if a participant is injured, or gets dirt in his eye, it is his opponent who comes to his aid – even with a $100,000 prize at stake.

23 Early Jul

❶ Turkey Tourism www.tourismturkey.org

Over 1,000 barefoot grapplers compete for Edirne's oil wrestling crown

10 Underwater Music Festival | NORTH AMERICA

Lower Keys, Florida, USA

While many orchestras perform under the stars, only one performs under the sea: a quirky concert unique to the Florida Keys that attracts an audience of 600 to North America's only living barrier reef. The Looe Key Marine Sanctuary, just south of Big Pine Key, plays host to the Lower Keys annual Underwater Music Festival – a sub-sea songfest amidst a colourful array of diverse marine life. Dive shops and private charters ferry concert-goers out to the Submerged Symphony - a one of-a-kind musical event at which snorkel, fins and flippers are de rigueur. Behind all the gimmicks, the festival carries a serious message of coral reef preservation. Diver awareness announcements, written and recorded by Florida Keys National Marine Sanctuary officials, pepper the musical broadcast.

📅 Saturday, Jul

ℹ️ Lower Keys Chamber of Commerce
www.lowerkeyschamber.com

Submerged symphonies typify Florida's underwater music festival

11 Boryeong Mud Festival | ASIA

South Korea

South Korea's Boryeong Mud Festival proves there is fun in filth. Three hours from Seoul, a 9.9 million square metre quagmire in Boryeong city offers an abundance of squidgy brown mud. Each July, around two-million locals and tourists let off steam on these sodden mineral-rich mudflats. When the festival began, in 1997, its aim was to promote Boryeong's mineral-rich mud used in skincare and beauty products. Today the nine-day Festival is a chance to drink beer and play dirty with sludge slides, mud-flinging, mock battles and bikini-clad mud wrestling babes – all clean fun in 200 tons of inky-green gunk.

📅 9-days, mid Jul

ℹ️ Boryeong Mud Festival www.mudfestival.or.kr
South Korea Tourism english.visitkorea.or.kr

12 Three Manly Games (Eriin Gurvan) | ASIA

Mongolia

Wrestling, horse racing and archery are the focus of the 'Three Manly Games" of Eriin Gurvan Naadam, a three-day highlight of the Mongolian year. Despite the name, the event is far from being exclusively macho; women take part in everything except wrestling. Daredevil displays of horsemanship are a major draw for Mongols who converge on Ulaanbaatar in their thousands.

📅 Mid Jul

ℹ Mongolia Tourism www.mongoliatourism.gov.mn

The core disciplines: wrestling, horse-racing and archery

13 Montreux Jazz Festival | EUROPE

Montreux, Switzerland

Since 1967, the Montreux Jazz Festival has been run with Swiss-style precision to offer everything from Brazilian rhythms to hardcore jazz. New acts and big names present a dazzling musical showcase of every imaginable style in a venue easily reached by dozens of surrounding cities. Keen to flee the crowds? Then give the main stages a miss and head to the Montreux Jazz Cafe – or, even better, the intimate gigs that take place on boats on the lake.

📅 Jul

ℹ www.montreuxjazz.com

14 Bastille Day Celebrations in Paris | EUROPE

Champs Elysées

France's republican zeal reaches fever pitch on Bastille Day, a festival commemorating the beginning of the French Revolution in 1789 when crowds stormed the Bastille prison - and the most important national holiday. On the evening of July 13th, crowds gather at Bastille Square in Paris for music and dancing while a huge military parade dominates morning festivities on the 14th. Led by the President, the procession, flanked by jets in formation, marches from the Arc de Triomphe to the Place de la Concorde. After dark, skies are illuminated by firework displays around the Eiffel Tower and Montparnasse.

📅 Jul 15th

ℹ Paris Tourist Office www.parisinfo.com

15 Rat Race

Edinburgh, Scotland

Edinburgh – or "Auld Reekie" as it is known to the locals – is renowned for its spine-tingling 1000-year history in which bloody battles, running amok and pride all played a part. Today, the city's rugged volcanic backdrop provides an instantly iconic starting point for the thrilling Rat Race - the UK's first-ever urban challenge. Since its inauguration in 2004, the Rat Race has brought the city to a halt on the 3rd Saturday in July as over 300 hardy types romp through the inner city on a two-day adventure using crampons, canoes and running shoes as the stopwatch ticks. The event involves running, walking, biking, kayaking, rope-related pursuits and orienteering together with a number of "secret tests" unveiled on the day.

🗓 3rd Saturday in July

ℹ Rat Race Edinburgh www.ratraceadventure.com

Edinburgh's testing Rat Race is the UK's first-ever urban challenge

16 Lumberjack Championships

Wisconsin

On the last weekend of July the Lumberjack Bowl in Hayward, Wisconsin hosts an annual spectacle of lumberjack prowess. Chopping, sawing, felling and log rolling are just some of the competitions that determine the Lumberjack World Champion in which the springboard chop, single bucking and river pigging are a major draw. More than 200 lumberjacks (and jills) showcase their skills in front of 12,000 spectators. The event dates back to 1960 and is now a part of ESPN's ultra-gutsy Great Outdoor Games.

🗓 Last weekend in Jul

ℹ World Lumberjack Championships

www.lumberjackworldchampionships.com

Lumberjack prowess is showcased during this annual spectacle

17 **Ernest Hemingway Festival** | NORTH AMERICA

Florida Keys, USA

Whether composing novels in his Whitehead Street, Key West writing studio or fishing for big game in local waters, Pulitzer Prize-winning author Ernest Hemingway left a powerful legacy in The Florida Keys, the 161 km (100 mile) necklace of islands that denote the Southernmost nub of the Continental USA. Today Hemingway's legacy remains an intrinsic part of the islands' cultural make-up with several shrines that pay homage to his passions, literary and otherwise. Crowds flock to Key West for author readings, book signings by grandson Edward Hemingway, an an exhibition of rare Hemingway memorabilia, and a short story contest directed by author and granddaughter Lorian Hemingway. A three-day marlin tournament honours his role as one of Key West's legendary salty old sea-dogs. In addition, Hemingway aficionados can view an ongoing exhibition of Hemingway family photographs, documents and memorabilia relating to the author's personal life in the island city at the Key West Museum of Art & History at the Custom House, 281 Front St.

However, it is the mid-July 'Papa Hemingway Look-Alike Contest' that stands out as an annual highlight, attracting over 100 stocky, bearded entrants – and the occasional female too. Since the first competition around 30 years ago, the event at Sloppy Joe's Bar – one of the late author's favourite watering holes – has drawn standing-room-only crowds. Would-be "Papas" can also take part in other festival activities, including an arm-wrestling contest and an infamous "Running of the Bulls" in which man-made bovine replicas rampage through Key West's streets cheered on by the crowds, in a zany salute to Pamplona's sporting challenge.

Dozens of bearded Papa look-alikes compete for the Hemingway medal

🗓 3 days, late Jul

ℹ Sloppy Joes Bar & Restaurant www.sloppyjoes.com
Florida Keys Tourism www.fla-keys.com

18 Love Parade

Berlin, Germany

Though synonymous with über-funky Berlin, the Love Parade moved its outlandish costumes and debauchery to Dortmund in 2008. Was it any more restrained? Not a bit, with everything you'd expect from the world's biggest street party and techno-fuelled dance orgy. From humble beginnings in 1989 - with one truck and 150 people - the Love Parade now transforms entire cities into a vast club scene overnight.

23 Jul

❶ Love Parade www.loveparade.de

Hedonists unite at Germany's techno-fuelled dance orgy

19 Gilroy Garlic Festival

California, USA

The locals of Gilroy swear they marinade a steak by simply pegging it out on a clothesline. Why? Because Gilroy is surrounded by garlic fields. For two decades Gilroy has honoured its favourite cooking pot ingredient with a garlic gala. Everything garlicky is celebrated with relish be it garlic fries (over 10,000 servings sold each year) or garlic ice cream. Worried about garlic breath? No need, free samples of breath freshener are handed out at every turn.

23 3 days, Jul

❶ Gilroy Garlic Festival gilroygarlicfestival.com

Mint anyone? Gilroy breath is assured at its annual garlic fest

20 Glyndebourne Opera | EUROPE

East Sussex, England

When founder John Christie, set up a professional opera house in England's rolling Sussex downs over 75 years ago his desire was to create something truly unique. Today, opera lovers from all over the world flock to the Glyndebourne Festival in the customary garb of black tie and evening dress for a summer extravaganza of stirring concertos and Champagne picnics under twinkling stars. Stroll around topiary-hemmed lawns and fountains edged by flowers before a bell signifies the curtain call. The state-of-the-art Opera House. is crafted out of century-old pitch pine and boasts truly astounding acoustics together with elegant curves illuminated by the soft glow of dozens of tiny lamps.

📅 May – Sep (Opera Season)
ℹ Glyndebourne Festival www.glyndebourne.com

21 Whitstable Oyster Festival | EUROPE

Kent, UK

For hundreds of years, the town of Whitstable has revolved around the sea. In Norman times the fishing port celebrated the feast day of St James of Compostella, the patron saint of oysters. After almost being wiped out in the 1920s by disease and overfishing, the oyster industry revived the lapsed celebrations of thanks for the riches of the sea. Today, on or around July 25th each year, a parade starts the nine-day jamboree with the official "Landing ofthe Catch" as oysters are ferried throughout the town on a horse-drawn dray followed by marching bands, revellers in period costumes, dance troupes and street entertainers – with plenty of local seafood stalls.

📅 9-days, Jul
ℹ Whitstable Oyster Festival
www.whitstableoysterfestival.co.uk

Expect olden feasting rituals at this oyster celebration

22 Twin Peaks Festival
NORTH AMERICA

North Bend, Seattle, USA

Set in North Bend, the town near Seattle where David Lynch made his seminal television series in the 1990s, this celebratory weekend-long festival includes hikes and bus trips to film locations and a Lynch movie night. Started in 1993, the Twin Peaks Festival attracts like-minded folk, who trade memorabilia and eat "Twin Peaks"-inspired food of cherry pie and damn fine coffee. Devotees dress up as their favourite Twin Peaks characters, swap stories, share insider info and compete in a fiercely-fought trivia contest. At least one actor from the series attends as a VIP guest.

23 Weekend, Jul

ℹ️ Twin Peaks Festival www.twinpeaksfest.com
Seattle Tourist Board www.visitseattle.org

23 Outdoor Cinema
EUROPE

Athens, Greece

At twilight, the ancient city of Athens yields to the dramatic illumination of the moon as shifting shadows cast their spell across soaring columns, mammoth archways and crumbling monuments. Sultry summer nights herald the arrival of the outdoor cinema season when more than 100 makeshift movie theatres swish open their curtains in the warm night air. Few movie-going experiences compare to this fine Athenian cinematic tradition where motion pictures entertain the crowds in leafy parks, backstreet gardens and rooftop terraces.

Movie-watching (kinema) al fresco debuted in Greece in the 19th century when short clips and newscasts were broadcast at dusk. Today, open-air cinemas in the city screen a wide range of homespun melodramas together with rare silent films, slush-and-trash B-movies and big-budget Hollywood spectacles - with the occasional 1950's retrospective thrown in for good measure (digitally re-mastered of course). Vintage black and white horror movies may lack the sophistication and special effects of modern bloodbath epics - but the spellbinding chill and tension they spark in an audience is palpable. From cheesy chick-flicks and comedic romps to art house, film noir and evocative drama - Athenians delight in the slightly grainy and jumpy retro film vibe. Simply climb the ramshackle steps to Cine Paris with a bean-bag, cushion or blanket (the last remaining seat in the house may be on bare ground) - but don't expect Multiplex-style gloss and glamour. Bygone cinematic in Athens is all about the clatter of vintage spooling, show-stopping power outages and a man selling roasted nuts from a broken lawn chair - how can an IMAX beat that?

23 Jun – Sep

ℹ️ Greek National Tourism Authority www.gnto.gr

24 Climbing Mt Fuji

| ASIA

Japan

As Japan's highest mountain, Fuji offers glorious views on a mild, clear day and during the two-month climbing season when the summit is free of snow Japanese and foreign hikers alike set off to for the 3,776-m (12,385-ft) summit. August is way too crowded as thousands begin a noisy ascent – forming queues on certain passes. July is much more tranquil with just the scenery as a distraction for trekkers with their eye on the top.

📅 Jul – Aug (free of heavy snow)
ℹ Japan Tourist Authority www.jnto.go.jp

Views are the only distraction on Mount Fuji on a clear, quiet day

25 Rafting the Kunene River

| AFRICA

Namibia

From November to March, the river of the Kunene valley begins to form white-topped crests between the cascades of Ruacana and Epupa Falls prompting great excitement in rafters and boarders. Forming a natural border between Angola and Namibia, the Kunene River is one of just five perennial rivers in arid Namibia, winding its way from Angola to the desolate Skeleton Coast and providing a precious resource for the people, plants and animals of the region. For almost 25 years preceding independence the river was out of bounds due to the perils of Namibia's bush war. In the early nineties, river adventure treks took off in a big way with a 120 km (74 mile) stretch of choppy water home to the surging Ondurusa rapids. Routes require rafters to paddle pass the looming Zebra Mountain before crossing "the Thirteen Rapids". On calmer stretches, crocodiles cautiously float towards passing rafts before sinking silently below the surface of the water. Striking scenery and bird life provide a backdrop to one of the last explored rivers in Southern Africa.

📅 Nov – Mar
ℹ www.namibiatourism.com.na

26 Calgary Stampede

Calgary, Canada

The first Calgary Stampede was held in 1912. Dubbed by enthusiasts the 'Greatest Outdoor Show on Earth', it wa founded by a local cowboy and vaudeville entertainer renowned for a traveling wild-west show. While the Stampede has grown and evolved, it retains the same western values. Prime attractions include rodeo, saddle bronc, bareback riding, parades, marching bands and western rider contests together with crazy clowns and wild cow-milking.

- 10 days, mid Jul
- Calgary Stampede www.calgarystampede.com
  Calgary Tourism www.tourismcalgary.com

Rodeo, roping and riding challenges determined wild-west grit

27 King's Peak

Utah, USA

Every summer, hundreds of adventurers aim for the top of King's Peak in the High Uinta Mountains – the highest point in Utah at 4,124 m (13,528 ft). Passes generally open up by late July and stay open through the month of August when a rough hike of around 15 miles still involves navigating high mountain passes cloaked in crunchy snow. Take the shortest route up Henry's Fork, from the North Slope, past sparking lakes, open alpine tundra and clumps of

stunted conifers and willow that are home to moose. A loose stone stretch and then it's a short scramble to the summit, marked by a tattered American flag – a rocky ledge provides a makeshift bench on which to perch and soak up jaw-dropping views.

- Jul - Aug (passes open early Jul and close Aug)
- Utah Tourism Council www.utah.com

28 Wildebeest Migration | AFRICA

Tanzania-Kenya

Every year, vast herds of over 1 million wildebeest migrate north from Tanzania's Serengeti National Park to Kenya's Masai Mara National Reserve in search of food. Travelling in column-shaped formations that stretch for miles, the wildebeest are joined by over half-a-million zebra and gazelle in a moving herd that is often referred to as the 'Greatest Show on Earth'. The dynamo behind the largest movement of wildlife on the planet is the region's rain-driven ecosystem: grasses are in short supply in the dry season so the wildebeest leave the depleted plains of the western part of the Serengeti in June to cross the mighty Grumeti and Mara Rivers. Vultures and Marabou storks line the banks in hungry anticipation as the wildebeest plunge into the river negotiating strong currents and crocodiles in their drive toward Kenya's well-nourished Masai Mara grasslands. A few months later, well-fed and watered by the short rains and bountiful grasslands, the wildebeest return to the sweet short-grass savannahs of the Serengeti National Park as light rains begin to fall.

Designated the eighth new wonder of the world, the wildebeest migration is an extraordinary spectacle on an epic scale - and arguably the most impressive natural event on land. In a region renowned for its big cats, elephants, crocodiles and birds of prey, predators are hot on the heels of the herd – with lion, hyena and cheetah the biggest threat. Other species include water, bush and reed buck, roan antelope, buffalo, spring hare, porcupine, warthog, hyraxes, baboon, vervet monkey, colobus monkey, patas monkey and mongoose. As grass provides little cover and young are easy pickings, wildebeest have evolved synchronized birthing. About 90 per cent of calves are born within a three week period around the same time as the zebra foaling season. Wildebeest young can run minutes after they are born – and within three days calves are strong enough to keep up with the herd.

📅 Jan – Jul

ℹ️ Serengeti National Park www.serengeti.org

Masai Mara Reserve www.maratriangle.org

29 The Mountains of the Moon | AFRICA

Uganda

Completely out of bounds during the rainy season, the Rwenzori Mountains form a 120 km (75 mile) spine along Uganda's western border. Dubbed the 'Mountains Of The Moon', the ridge is frequently cloaked in misty cloud with a half-dozen peaks carrying permanent snow, three with glaciers. The highest of these peaks, and the third highest peak in Africa, is Mt. Margherita rising 5,102 m (16, 740 ft)

above sea level amidst resplendent rainforest, giant heather, waterfalls, butterfly-filled swamps and lakes. Visit when "dry" (less boggy) July to mid-September.

📅 Mar – Jul (dry season)

ℹ️ Ugandan Wildlife Authority www.uwa.or.ug/rwenzori.html

Uganda Tourism www.visituganda.com

30 Barefoot Festival and Goddess Camp | EUROPE

Leicestershire, England

Set in a farmer's field in Leicestershire, the three-day Barefoot Festival and Goddess Camp celebrates the divine through dance, movement, music and spiritual healing, holistic therapies, massage, meditation and a chill out zone. The festival enjoys stunning views of the beautiful Soar Valley. Join meditation workshops, enjoy belly dance class or simply chill out.

📅 3 days, end of Jul
ℹ Barefoot Festival & Goddess Camp, Leicester
www.goddess-camp.com

31 Mumbai Xpress | ASIA

India

India's insane 1,000 km (1,180 mile) Mumbai Xpress Rickshaw Challenge pays homage to the country's unofficial national vehicle. The race kicks off in Chennai (Madras), the automobile capital of India – an ironic touch given that India's three-wheeled, two-stroke motorized rickshaws are without seatbelts, windows or doors and prone to mechanical mishap. Over a dozen teams of more than 50 people include participants from the UK, US, Poland, Hungary, Russia and Australia. Each is competing to cross the finishing line first in Kanyakumari on India's southern-most tip. In intrepid style, they will battle monsoon rains, rutted roads, crowds, wildlife and other typical Indian obstacles through every possible micro-climate; from metropolis, tropical jungle, arid desert, ancient valleys and coastline. The race is strictly fun, without any prize at the chequered flag. Each participant pays around 1,500 euros to enter. Given the vehicular challenges of India's temperamental three-wheeler, a team of mechanics follow the rally with a toolkit for essential repairs. Most participants have never driven the subcontinent's iconic tuk tuk before they start the engine in a bid to speed across Tamil Nadu, Karnataka, Goa, and Maharashtra. Spewing fumes at a top speed of 80 km (50 miles) per hour, India's rickshaws first rolled off the production line in 1957 and have remained almost entirely unchanged, boasting a sheet-metal body, a canvass roof – and a teeny turning circle that allows it to weave through congested traffic.

📅 14 days Aug – Jul
ℹ Mumbai Xpress rickshawchallenge.com
India Tourism www.incredibleindia.org

August

1 Shoton Festival

Tibet

Meaning yoghurt banquet, the festival of Shoton dates back to the 11th century. To celebrate the end of a month of meditation by the monks local residents would bring alms of yoghurt to the monasteries. In the early 18th century, the main Shoton celebrations were moved to Norbu Lingka – the summer palace of the Dalai Lama. Today festivities involve vast banquets with fresh, creamy yoghurt and operatic concerts from the first to the fifth of the seventh month in the Tibetan calendar.

📅 First day of the seventh month of the Tibetan year
ℹ️ China National Tourist Office www.cnto.org

2 Gay Pride

Amsterdam, Holland

Amsterdam's annual three-day Gay Pride is held in mid-summer in one of the world's most liberal-minded cities. Only the broad-minded attend Friday's kick-off street party, zoned across various sectors of the city, e.g.: Fetish, Blondes, Muscles, Trendy and Leather. Over 350,000 spectators line Prinsengracht and Amstel Rivers for Saturday's famous afternoon Canal Parade when dozens of highly-decorated and amusingly-outrageous floats entertain the crowd. Sunday's afternoon closing party is followed by umpteen riotous after-parties that rage 'til dawn.

📅 Late Jul, early Aug – 7 days
ℹ️ Amsterdam Gay Pride www.amsterdamgaypride.nl
   Amsterdam Tourist Office www.amsterdamtourist.nl

Riotous parties and outlandish costumes are central to Amsterdam's celebration of gayness

3 Parkour

Moscow, Russia

Part extreme sport, part meditative challenge, Moscow's cult-status parkour craze encourages gruelling discipline, self-improvement and interdependence. Aficionados ooze the honed confidence of ardent training, rocking back on one foot, poised to snap into action with fingertips hooked onto high-rise ledges. They may be all shapes, ages and sizes, but they share a common desire to run unencumbered and unhindered through urban space. Is this an expression of a basic human urge for freedom in an oppressive suburban environment? So say psychologists. Yet most practitioners simply consider it as moving in the least energy-consuming way from A to B using just the abilities of the body. Local club, the Moscow Tracers encourages fans to look beyond the Internet clips lest the Eastern-inspired philosophy become lost in digital high-jinx. Free-running meet-ups take place in several city hotspots, beginning with a full stretch and warm up at City University.

Customary hurdles on the University campus include fences, walls, railings, stairwells, rubbish skips and rooftop chasms with plenty of exhilarating gravity-defying trails to test the precision of mind and body. Try stairwell jumps, propelling climbs and crawls before an ultra-graceful cat-jump (in which the exponent places two hands on an obstacle and leaps between them). Then maybe a tic-tac (a kind-of push-off made mid-movement from a wall or other hurdle), a speed vault, turn-vault, under-bar and monkey vault – each requiring gasp-inducing agility.

Summer (Jun - Sep)

Russia Tourist Board www.visitrussia.org.uk

Stairwell jumps, push-offs and rooftop chasms test the mind and body

August

4 World Bog Snorkelling Championships | EUROPE

Llanwrtyd Wells, Powys, Wales

Prepare to get cold, wet and covered from head to toe in peaty, thick, black sludge at the World Bog Snorkelling Championships, held every August in Powys in Wales. Said to be the brainchild of the local Powys villagers after too much Welsh ale in 1986, the event now attracts competitors from as far away as Australia. Llanwrtyd Wells is renowned for its murky weed-tangled marshlands. Two 55 m (180 ft) trenches, cut each year, provide the race-track for this messy sprint in which swimmers in full snorkel garb (wetsuit, flippers and mask) are timed over a two-length dash. Dubbed 'dirty fun in Waen Rhydd Bog' the Championships may be a summer fixture, but that doesn't stop the relentless Welsh rain. Water levels rise, creating a slushy stew rich in antioxidants, wriggling worms and bugs.

Beating the suction is tricky and swallowing the boggy slime inevitable – but all unpleasant ingestion experiences en route are quickly forgotten with a year's worth of ice cream up for grabs as the prize. At just over 1 minute 35 seconds, beating the current World Record requires steely determination, stamina and focus with over a hundred contestants each year from 14-year-old school boys and 70-year-old grandmothers to athletes with their eye on gold. Optional fancy dress ensures the race is a riot of pyjamas, togas, Hawaiian shirts and Welsh national dress. Four categories offer a world, women's, junior and local championship title. All proceeds are donated to charities and good causes in the region. Rules prohibit all recognizable swimming strokes so a wild style of doggy paddle proves the most popular style of propulsion.

 Weekend in Aug

 Visit Powys www.tourism.powys.gov.uk

Getting down and dirty: Powy's Bog Snorkelling Championships

5 Tooth Festival

Kandy, Sri Lanka

Buddha's upper canine tooth is said to be stored in a 17th-century Sri Dalada Maligawa temple in Kandy, Sri Lanka's long-established centre of the Buddhist faith. Vast numbers of pilgrims journey to be near this precious relic in August each year, clad from head-to-toe in white and bearing lotus blossoms and fragrant frangipani. The tooth is removed from its shrine for this one occasion, marked by a spectacular 10-day torchlight parade. Fire dancers fend off curses during the Esala Perahera Festival while whip-cracking torch-bearers clear a path through crowds of over a million people, followed by 100 ornately decorated elephants, throngs of musicians, jugglers, dancers, drummers, acrobats and Buddhist devotees together with members of noble families in Ceylonese garb.

🗓 10-days, Jul - Aug

ℹ Sri Lankan Tourism Authority www.srilankatourism.org

6 Great British Beer Festival

London, England

August is scribed in every beer lover's diary when Earl's Court in the heart of genteel West London hosts the Great British Beer Festival, organized by the Campaign for Real Ale (CAMRA), guardians of The British Pint. Over five days, several thousand beer drinkers sup more than 450 good-quality brews from breweries large and small in a makeshift bar the size of an aircraft hangar. Simply pluck a plastic cup to taste a wide range of beers from Welsh Pale Ales and earthy English bitters to barley wines and creamy-rich Irish stouts. Expert panels judge the hotly contested Champion Beer of Britain competition.

Tutored tasting sessions are available to teach the curious how to recognize the tens of distinct flavours that go to make up the perfect pint and sort out the the Dogbolters from the Doombars and Dark Espresso Stout brews. Aside from the beer, revellers can partake in traditional British pub pursuits such as a skittles contest and fiendishly difficult pub quizzes, as well as munch on gourmet versions of traditional pub fare such as pork scratchings and pickled eggs. Whatever you do, don't ask for a pilsner.

Over 450 good-quality beers range from pale ales to creamy stouts

🗓 5-days, early Aug

ℹ CAMRA (Campaign for Real Ale) www.camra.org.uk
   Visit London www.visitlondon.com

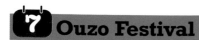

7 Ouzo Festival
| EUROPE

Plomari, Greece

Plomarian's have the reputation of enjoying life to the full – and much of this merriment centres on the town's free-flowing local grog. Using traditional distilling methods to create extra strong potency, Plomari's anise-flavoured spirit is the certified drink of revolution, freedom and love. The festival (or 'panigiri') season kicks off with a lively celebration of Plomari's ouzo with umpteen stalls offering generous samples of the local tipple – many up to 46 per cent alcohol.

📅 Late Jul - early Aug
ℹ Plomari City Touirsm www.plomaricity.gr
  Greece Tourist Office www.gnto.gr

8 Costa Maya Festival
| SOUTH AMERICA

San Pedro, Belize

In the first week of August, Belize cuts loose to celebrate the biggest annual festival in Central America with big-name musical acts, non-stop dancing and lots of beautiful girls in skimpy swimwear. Belize's sizzling La Reina de la Costa Maya pageant draws crowds of entertainers, spectators and contestants to a pretty palm-scattered beach in San Pedro. Expect beer, boiled shrimp and bikini-clad babes in abundance together with some first-rate folkloric shows and local crafts.

📅 Mid-Aug, 7-days
ℹ Costa Maya Festival www.costamayafestival.com
  Belize Tourism www.belizetourism.org

9 Pearl Diving Festival (Qafal)
| ASIA

Kuwait

For two-decades, the Kuwait Pearl Diving Festival (Qafal) has commemorated the rich traditions of a pre-oil era when pearls provided the economic bedrock on which Kuwaiti wealth was built. Held each Aug, the festival recognizes the courage of pearl divers in a month-long celebration. Volunteers from Kuwait's sea-faring and fishing families undergo intensive training in deep-dive tactics, neck baskets (dieng) and toe anchors (hajer) to replicate ancient ways to search for exquisite pearls.

📅 Aug
ℹ Kuwait Tourism www.kuwaittourism.com

Ghost Festival | ASIA

...roots in Buddhism, China's Ghost Festival is a ...occasion, symbolizing the links between the ...nd the dead, earth and heaven, body and soul. ...g the end of Ghost Month (the seventh month ...Chinese calendar), the festival is the climax to ...d when ghosts and spirits are believed to ...e from the lower world to visit Earth. A day of ...when people offer gifts of food to the spirits, ...tival is also a time to burn paper money for ...ncestors.

...ival marks end of month-long observance

...na National Tourist Office www.china.org.cn

Solemn rituals honour dead ancestors

Night of the Shooting Stars | EUROPE

...aises a glass in toast to the 'Night of the ...ting Stars' at over 200 of the country's wine-...icing towns in the hope that wishes made on ...ng star will come true. On an evening in mid-...st, around a million visitors from far and wide ...skyward with a wine-filled goblet in hand in ...ing locations carefully chosen to heighten the

shooting star spectacle. Castles, medieval plazas and hilltop vineyards provide a magical setting. Artificial lights are extinguished in order to showcase the dazzle of falling stars to music and poetry recitals.

📅 Mid Aug

ℹ️ Italian Tourist Board www.italiantouristboard.co.uk

Seoul Fringe Festival | ASIA

...ea

...two-week celebration of independent, ...erground and often just weird and bizarre art, ...ic and theatre is a wholly unpredictable feast. ...ormances, exhibits, films and concerts seem ...appen at whim in the dozens of small theatres, ...lubs and galleries near Hong-Ik University in ...gdae, Seoul. The high-energy Seoul Fringe Festival

provides an exciting not-to-be-missed opportunity to 'discover' 300 independent and cool Korean and international artists on the up.

📅 2 weeks mid-Aug

ℹ️ Seoul Fringe Festival www.seoulfringefestival.net
Seoul Tourism www.visitseoul.net

10 Night Golf | ASIA

Nad al Sheba, Dubai

August sees temperatures soar in desert-settled Dubai where the mercury hit a scorching 47.5°C (117.5°F) in 1999. Once the seasonal dust storms have subsided to a weak-willed breeze, humidity can be oppressive with the comfort index shooting up to 8 - a 'near stress' reading. Being outside for longer than 10 minutes at a time in daylight can be extremely uncomfortable, yet golfers will find it more than possible to enjoy a pleasant round of golf at Nad al Sheba - home to Dubai's prestigious night golf.

Built along similar lines to St Andrews in Scotland, the golf course is constructed in and around the Nad al Sheba racetrack, host of the world's richest horse race, the $US 6 million Dubai World Cup. Designed in the classic Scottish links style with eight lakes and more than 110 deep pot bunkers, the 18-hole Nad al Sheba requires accurate hitting rather than length, with elevated tees on the back nine offering stunning views across this beautiful grassy course. Flawless greens are the result of a million litres of water, pumped through a state-of-the-art irrigation system in the wee small hours once the last golfer has packed up his clubs for the night.

Nad al Sheba's golf course is open until midnight and boasts extensive floodlighting to allow a first-class round after dark. A Golf Academy run by four British PGA Golf Professionals offers tuition for all abilities, including a popular 'learn golf in a week' course taught in small groups. Out on the fairways, testing water hazards provide formidable protection to both nines - although the biggest challenge to night players here could well be finding a ball in the sand-scrub rough. The distance it travels over Bermuda-hybrid grass and hot desert sand can be very deceptive in dusty gusts - so sales of day-glow balls in the Pro Shop do a roaring trade.

📅 Year-round (though best in the sweltering heat of summer when the coolest hours are after dark)

ℹ️ Dubai Tourism www.dubaitourism.ae

Enjoy the cool of the fairways after dark at floodlit Nad al Sheba

11 Vel Festival

Colombo, Sri Lanka

Vel takes place between Colombo's Hindu temples in Sea Street and Bambalapitiya in honour of war god, Lord Murukan. A gilded carriage drawn by a pair of groomed white bulls travels along streets decorated with palm fronds. Drums resound and bells tinkle in a procession marked by divine songs. At the temple, thousands of devotees pay their respects by smashing coconuts, burning incense and igniting camphor. Stalls line the roads – beads, bangles, candy, pottery, drinks and snacks attract religious and non-believer alike to this colourful celebration of good triumphing over the forces of evil.

📅 Jul or Aug

ℹ Sri Lanka Tourism www.srilankatourism.org

Thousands of devotees banish evil spirits in honour of the war god

12 Fjord Swimming

EUROPE

Sognefjord, Norway

Unlike the rest of the year, water temperatures in Norway's deepest and longest fjord in the west coast of country reach a still-chilly 15°C (59°F) in August. Dubbed the 'King of fjords', Sognefjord is at the epicentre of Norway's fjord swimming mania that sees strong swimmers navigate 900 m (3,000 ft)-deep waters amid spectacular 900 m (3,000 ft) mountains. In August, competitors from all over the world compete in a 3.7 km (2.3 mile) Sognefjorden Challenge . The field is strictly limited to 30 confident swimmers on a route which passes through narrow, glacier-carved straights.

📅 Jun - end of Aug

ℹ Norway Tourism www.visitnorway.com

Navigate deep cliff-topped fjords marvelling at the panoramic view

13 Birding in the Danube Delta

Romania

The Romanian Danube Delta comprises 23 natural ecosystems and floating reed islands. Large lakes, ponds, streamlets and rivers are home to 300 bird species with around 45 freshwater fish species in the lagoons and marshes. In 1991, the delta gained UNESCO World Heritage status with 2,733 sq km (1,055 sq mile) protected areas. Floating pontoons and viewing platforms offer exce with pelicans, herons and cormor amidst one of Europe's finest bio

📅 Aug

ℹ Romanian Tourist Board www.roman
Romanian Ornithological Society ww

14 Edinburgh Fringe Festival

Scotland

More than 31,300 performers from 47 countries appear in over 2,000 shows during the five frantic weeks of the Edinburgh Fringe Festival – with 1.7 million tickets sold. A third of the programme is comedy; almost a third is theatre; and 17 per cent is music – with rest a mishmash of opera, dance, children's shows, theatre and exhibitions. Performances take place in an eclectic range of venues across the city from several thousand seater auditoriums to tiny rooms with only a few audience members present. Launched in 1947 as the sibling upstart of the Edinburgh International Festival, the Fringe has grown to eclipse the original event. Over the years, many of Britain's most famous comedians and performers have made their name at the Fringe, and festival goers are often the first to witness seminal turns by stars of the future.

📅 3 weeks, Aug

ℹ Edinburgh Fringe Festival www.edfringe.com

Over 1.7 million tickets sold for Edinburgh's five wil

Chir

With
soler
living
Mark
of th
a pe
eme
pray
the
dea

📅

ℹ

It
It
S
F

10 Night Golf

Nad al Sheba, Dubai

August sees temperatures soar in desert-settled Dubai where the mercury hit a scorching 47.5°C (117.5°F) in 1999. Once the seasonal dust storms have subsided to a weak-willed breeze, humidity can be oppressive with the comfort index shooting up to 8 - a 'near stress' reading. Being outside for longer than 10 minutes at a time in daylight can be extremely uncomfortable, yet golfers will find it more than possible to enjoy a pleasant round of golf at Nad al Sheba - home to Dubai's prestigious night golf.

Built along similar lines to St Andrews in Scotland, the golf course is constructed in and around the Nad al Sheba racetrack, host of the world's richest horse race, the $US 6 million Dubai World Cup. Designed in the classic Scottish links style with eight lakes and more than 110 deep pot bunkers, the 18-hole Nad al Sheba requires accurate hitting rather than length, with elevated tees on the back nine offering stunning views across this beautiful grassy course. Flawless greens are the result of a million litres of water, pumped through a state-of-the-art irrigation system in the wee small hours once the last golfer has packed up his clubs for the night.

Nad al Sheba's golf course is open until midnight and boasts extensive floodlighting to allow a first-class round after dark. A Golf Academy run by four British PGA Golf Professionals offers tuition for all abilities, including a popular 'learn golf in a week' course taught in small groups. Out on the fairways, testing water hazards provide formidable protection to both nines - although the biggest challenge to night players here could well be finding a ball in the sand-scrub rough. The distance it travels over Bermuda-hybrid grass and hot desert sand can be very deceptive in dusty gusts - so sales of day-glow balls in the Pro Shop do a roaring trade.

📅 Year-round (though best in the sweltering heat of summer when the coolest hours are after dark)

ℹ Dubai Tourism www.dubaitourism.ae

Enjoy the cool of the fairways after dark at floodlit Nad al Sheba

11 Vel Festival | ASIA

Colombo, Sri Lanka

Vel takes place between Colombo's Hindu temples in Sea Street and Bambalapitiya in honour of war god, Lord Murukan. A gilded carriage drawn by a pair of groomed white bulls travels along streets decorated with palm fronds. Drums resound and bells tinkle in a procession marked by divine songs. At the temple, thousands of devotees pay their respects by smashing coconuts, burning incense and igniting camphor. Stalls line the roads – beads, bangles, candy, pottery, drinks and snacks attract religious and non-believer alike to this colourful celebration of good triumphing over the forces of evil.

Thousands of devotees banish evil spirits in honour of the war god

📅 Jul or Aug

ℹ Sri Lanka Tourism www.srilankatourism.org

12 Fjord Swimming | EUROPE

Sognefjord, Norway

Unlike the rest of the year, water temperatures in Norway's deepest and longest fjord in the west coast of country reach a still-chillly 15°C (59°F) in August. Dubbed the 'King of fjords', Sognefjord is at the epicentre of Norway's fjord swimming mania that sees strong swimmers navigate 900 m (3,000 ft)-deep waters amid spectacular 900 m (3,000 ft) mountains. In August, competitors from all over the world compete in a 3.7 km (2.3 mile) Sognefjorden Challenge . The field is strictly limited to 30 confident swimmers on a route which passes through narrow, glacier-carved straights.

📅 Jun - end of Aug

ℹ Norway Tourism www.visitnorway.com

Navigate deep cliff-topped fjords marvelling at the panoramic view

13 Birding in the Danube Delta

Romania

The Romanian Danube Delta comprises 23 natural ecosystems and floating reed islands. Large lakes, ponds, streamlets and rivers are home to 300 bird species with around 45 freshwater fish species in the lagoons and marshes. In 1991, the delta gained UNESCO World Heritage status with 2,733 sq km (1,055 sq mile) protected areas. Floating pontoons and viewing platforms offer excellent birding spots – with pelicans, herons and cormorants in August – amidst one of Europe's finest biosphere reserves.

📅 Aug

ℹ Romanian Tourist Board www.romaniatourism.com
Romanian Ornithological Society www.sor.ro

14 Edinburgh Fringe Festival

Scotland

More than 31,300 performers from 47 countries appear in over 2,000 shows during the five frantic weeks of the Edinburgh Fringe Festival – with 1.7 million tickets sold. A third of the programme is comedy; almost a third is theatre; and 17 per cent is music – with rest a mishmash of opera, dance, children's shows, theatre and exhibitions. Performances take place in an eclectic range of venues across the city from several thousand seater auditoriums to tiny rooms with only a few audience members present. Launched in 1947 as the sibling upstart of the Edinburgh International Festival, the Fringe has grown to eclipse the original event. Over the years, many of Britain's most famous comedians and performers have made their name at the Fringe, and festival goers are often the first to witness seminal turns by stars of the future.

📅 3 weeks, Aug

ℹ Edinburgh Fringe Festival www.edfringe.com

Over 1.7 million tickets sold for Edinburgh's five wild days of comedy

15 Ghost Festival

ASIA

China

With its roots in Buddhism, China's Ghost Festival is a solemn occasion, symbolizing the links between the living and the dead, earth and heaven, body and soul. Marking the end of Ghost Month (the seventh month of the Chinese calendar), the festival is the climax to a period when ghosts and spirits are believed to emerge from the lower world to visit Earth. A day of prayer when people offer gifts of food to the spirits, the festival is also a time to burn paper money for dead ancestors.

23 Festival marks end of month-long observance

❶ China National Tourist Office www.china.org.cn

Solemn rituals honour dead ancestors

16 Night of the Shooting Stars

EUROPE

Italy

Italy raises a glass in toast to the 'Night of the Shooting Stars' at over 200 of the country's wine-producing towns in the hope that wishes made on a falling star will come true. On an evening in mid-August, around a million visitors from far and wide gaze skyward with a wine-filled goblet in hand in stunning locations carefully chosen to heighten the shooting star spectacle. Castles, medieval plazas and hilltop vineyards provide a magical setting. Artificial lights are extinguished in order to showcase the dazzle of falling stars to music and poetry recitals.

23 Mid Aug

❶ Italian Tourist Board www.italiantouristboard.co.uk

17 Seoul Fringe Festival

ASIA

Korea

This two-week celebration of independent, underground and often just weird and bizarre art, music and theatre is a wholly unpredictable feast. Performances, exhibits, films and concerts seem to happen at whim in the dozens of small theatres, art clubs and galleries near Hong-Ik University in Hongdae, Seoul. The high-energy Seoul Fringe Festival provides an exciting not-to-be-missed opportunity to 'discover' 300 independent and cool Korean and international artists on the up.

23 2 weeks mid-Aug

❶ Seoul Fringe Festival www.seoulfringefestival.net

Seoul Tourism www.visitseoul.net

18 Funghi Foraging

Poland

Poles become preoccupied with the forests from mid summer to late autumn as the country's mushroom gathering season gets underway. Even the simplest country stroll becomes a major foraging expedition as mushroom hunters scour Poland's natural larders for fungi in all shapes, sizes and hues. Many are sold at local markets or are dried, bottled and deep-frozen in a fungi frenzy – with the deep-flavoured borowik mushroom the most-prized of them all.

📅 Mid-Aug to early Oct
ℹ Polish National Tourist Office www.polandtour.org

Autumn is a foraging frenzy in the mushroom-rich forests of Poland

19 Norwegian Trolls

Andalsnes, Norway

In Norwegian mythology, the troll is believed to hide in caves and riverbanks in wilderness terrains. Troll-related Nordic folklore is especially prevalent in Andalsnes, a village squeezed between craggy peaks and the fjords. As a gateway to some truly dramatic scenery, Andalsenes is launch point for Trollveggen (Troll Wall) – Europe's highest rock massif at 1,800 m (5,600 ft). Trolldom (Troll Magic), Trollkjerringa (Trolls Wife) and the hair-raising hairpin bends of Trollstigen (Troll's Path) – and in summer, Norway's practitioners of mischief are said to hide amidst waterfalls with tomfoolery in mind.

📅 Summer (Jun - end of Aug)
ℹ Norway Tourism www.visitnorway.com

Mischievous troll tomfoolery characterizes Nordic mythology

20 Olive Festival

Paso Robles, California, USA

As California's third largest wine-producing region, Paso Robles is surrounded by vines – yet tucked amongst the terraces are the area's lesser-known olive groves. Paso Robles may play a small role in California's century-old olive-producing sector (99.9 per cent of America's home-grown olive oil hails from the state) but it is immensely proud of its olive groves. An annual festival celebrates the humble olive in the Downtown City Park attracting thousands of locals and olive aficionados alike. The Paso Robles olive boasts a nutty flavour and there are numerous opportunities to try them at the Olive Festival. Stalls sell a host of mouth-watering delights from tree-ripened olives, dried olives and pesto to oils. Non-food displays pay homage to 'everything olive' – such as soaps, body oils and olive-scented candles.

Traditionally, olives are grown on the fringes of the Mediterranean, although California now accounts for more than 65,000 tons a year. Scarcely bigger than a baked bean when harvested, the olives are inedible, their bitter astringency has to be removed by saline soaking. Fruit are washed, with leaves and twigs removed, before being placed into 50 kg (110 lb) sacks – not all the fruit on an olive tree is ready for gathering at the same time and pickers will return to a tree many times during a harvest. Paso Robles produces a clear yellow-green blend from Mission, Arbequina, and Tuscan olive varieties – fruit for oil production is taken as soon as it reaches optimum ripeness when it will yield the maximum oil with the most flavour. Flavours differ from oil to oil and are influenced by the quality and composition of the soil. The timing of the harvest is also paramount – much like the grapes of Paso Robles.

Pay homage to all things olivey from pesto and soaps to tree-ripened frui

📅 Late Aug

ℹ Paso Robles Olive Festival www.pasoolivefestival.com

21 Heilala Week

Tongatapu, Tonga

Tonga's main island Tongatapu stages the Heilala Week Festival (mid-July to late August) in honour of the national flower, which blooms around this time. Most of the festivities centre on the capital city Nuku'alofa where highlights include a Miss Heilala pageant together with live music and parties. A fine exhibition of local handicrafts dominates the city but it is the grand flower-filled Float Parade that draws the crowds on Saturday afternoon.

📅 1-week, Jul – Aug
ℹ Royal Kingdom of Tonga Tourism www.vacations.tvb.gov.to

22 Parma Ham Festival

Parma, Italy

Every weekend from late August through September Parma's farms and factories throw open their doors to allow passersby to taste the wares. Parma ham has a slightly nutty flavour and this fine, aged, dry-cured meat can be found in abundance in over a dozen small towns to the south of the city. Visit numerous parma ham factories together with dozens of restaurants that specialize in the local prosciutto dishes – there's also a Museo del Prosciutto in a former cattle market for hardcore ham connoisseurs.

📅 End of Aug to mid - late Sep
ℹ Parma Ham Festival www.festivaldelprosciuttodiparma.com

23 Sunset at Khan Tengri

Kyrgyzstan

Located on the Kyrgyz-Chinese border in the heart of the Central Tian Shan (Mountains of Heaven), Khan Tengri forms the highest point on the Tengri Tag sub-range between the Northern and Southern Inylchek Glaciers. At sunset, the marble-rich main summit boasts a deep red glow, giving the 7,000 m (23,000 ft) peak its Kazakh name "Kan Tau" – meaning "Blood Mountain." A short climbing season from mid-July to late August means this great challenge is often over-looked. Those that reach the top not only experience a truly unforgettable sunset, but also can bury a message in a capsule in the soil that contains words of congratulations from climbers through the ages.

A deep red shroud glows around the main summit at sunset

📅 Mid-Jul to late Aug (climbing season)
ℹ Adventure Peaks www.adventurepeaks.com

24 Shakespeare at the Collector

Arundel, West Sussex, England

Each year, the British Shakespeare Company sets the handsome Collector Earl's Garden alight at beautiful Arundel Castle in West Sussex across a four-day event performed in Elizabethan costume. Resplendent colour and contemporary horticultural themes characterize the Collector Earl's Garden – a lush, backdrop to an open-air festival of Shakespearean classics performed by some of Britain's finest professional Shakespearian actors. Arundel Castle sits high on a hill, dominating the landscape, with magnificent views across the South Downs and the River Arun.

📅 Late Aug

ℹ️ British Shakespeare Company
   www.britishshakespearecompany.com
   Arundel Castle www.arundelcastle.org

25 Burning Man Festival

Nevada, USA

Don't bother scouring a map for the town of Black Rock City – this desert township of 50,000 souls north of Reno in Nevada only exists for a week once a year. Set in stunning middle-of-nowhere seclusion, Black Rock City has a single function: to host the annual Burning Man arts festival and bacchanal at the end of August. Boasting near-mythical status, Burning Man is no ordinary arts event. Described as a mix between New Year, Marti Gras, Halloween, the 4th of July, and the Apocalypse – all rolled into one – the festival is famous for its 'free range art' with everything from absurd installations and spray-painted trucks to eco trash-can sculpture. The Burning Man is unique in that most of the art is burned – a tribute to the originator of the festival. In 1986, Larry Harvey, a jilted lover, drove to San Francisco beach to burn a wooden effigy of the man he wished to cease being. Today, a similarly styled 12 m (40 ft) wooden figure stands tall at the centre of the clock-face-shaped temporary city and is ignited on Saturday night as a powerful climax to one of the most kaleidoscopic and alternative art-fests on the planet.

Burning an effigy signals the climax of this annual gathering

📅 Aug (week prior and including Labor Day)

ℹ️ Nevada Tourism travelnevada.com

26 Notting Hill Carnival

London

Festival-goers at London's two-day Notting Hill Carnival are a hungry bunch, consuming 70,000 litres (150,000 pints) of carrot juice, five tons of chicken, 300,000 corn cobs, 12,000 mangoes and a ton of Jamaican patties – washed down with 10,000 litres (21,000 pints) of Caribbean stout and 25,000 bottles of rum. Over 750,000 spectators cram the streets for the parade of 70 costumed bands and dozens of highly-decorated floats. Originally an offshoot of the Trinidad Carnival in 1964, the Notting Hill Carnival has remained true to its Caribbean roots. On August Bank Holiday weekend, a three-mile route is punctuated by 40 sound systems pumping out African beats, Calypso and reggae.

📅 Bank Holiday Weekend Aug (end of the month)
ℹ www.nottinghillcarnival.org.uk

27 La Tomatina

Buñol, Spain

Home to the world's biggest tomato fight (La Tomatina), Buñol in Valencia is a sleepy provincial town which erupts into a frenzied mush of red squishy splat every summer. Everyone gets messy during the massive tomato battle in Buñol's main town square, a traditional skirmish dating back to the 1940s when a simple act of rowdiness got out of hand. Today, the good people gather under the clock tower to lob tomatoes at any moving target – an annual ritual on the last Wednesday of every August that has grown exponentially over the years.

📅 Last Wed in Aug
ℹ La Tomantina Festival www.latomatina.es

28 La Fiesta Major de Gràcia

Barcelona, Spain

Every year at the Fiesta Major de Gràcia in Barcelona, a group of sinister, dark costumed 'correfoc' (devils) run amok amongst the crowds. However it is the music, fireworks, street food and dancing that provide the main focal point of this colourful celebration – where the merriment goes on and on. Officially, Gracia's concerts and street theatre run for only six days – but the revelry lasts longer than that.

📅 Last half of Aug
ℹ www.festamajordegracia.cat

Art dominates the streets of this Barcelonan suburb

29 Aarhus Festival | EUROPE

Denmark

A major event in Denmark's calendar, the Aarhus Festival paralyses normal life in the town for 10 lively days. Founded in 1965, the August festival has a very wide artistic remit with over 300 imaginative events. Highlights include a fabulous programme of music, from big-name international rock bands and acoustic solo artists to traditional music and native dance.

Events take place in venues all over Aarhus. Contemporary exhibitions showcase a dizzying array of sculpture, photography and crafts together with lots of fun-filled activities for kids.

📅 Last Friday in Aug
ℹ Denmark Tourism www.visitdenmark.com

30 Whale Watching in Newfoundland | NORTH AMERICA

Canada

Canadians swear there is no better place to come face to face with a humpback whale than in Newfoundland where no fewer than 22 species of ocean mammals can be spotted – not just from boats on the water but from dry land too (great for those with wobbly sea legs). Daredevil whale watchers can even hire a kayak to paddle alongside these magnificent creatures of the deep – a thrilling marine encounter. A whale's moan is louder than a Boeing 747 jumbo jet on take-off with the songs of male humpbacks the longest and most complex in the entire animal world. As the boat bounces full-throttle out to open waters, it is common for bottlenose dolphins to bow-ride alongside the boat in sleek synchronization. Whales feed in the nutrient-rich waters along the Newfoundland coast with humpback, minke, pilot, orca, fin, sperm and blue whales a major draw. As a glistening arched back and dorsal fin rise high above the surface cry "thar she blows" Captain Ahab-style: few superlatives can match the moment. Then, in a split second, the king of the ocean is gone, a towering spume of misty water all that is left in its wake.

Twenty-two species of marine mammal can be spotted here

📅 May - Sep (best Jun & Aug)
ℹ Newfoundland Tourism www.newfoundlandlabrador.com

31 Indoor Skiing

Dubai

Despite soaring temperatures that can top 45°C (113°F), Dubai's desert terrain still manages to boast several inches of snow. Creating an Alpine winter wonderland in an arid region without hills posed little problem to the sun-baked emirate – it is, after all, the home of temperature-controlled beaches and manmade islands. Dubbed "the coolest thing in Dubai," the project cost $US 272 million to complete and is the first of its kind in the Middle East – hardly surprising given the climatic challenges this meteorological oddity presents. Over 6,000 tons of snow covers the 22.5 sq km (18.5 sq miles) slope (the size of three football pitches) where temperatures are maintained to a meticulous –1°C (30°F) all year round. Ski Dubai can comfortably accommodate 1,500 skiers, snowboarders and toboggan-riders and allows visitors the opportunity to slalom in boots, gloves and thermal coats between bouts of sunbathing in the ferocious midday sun. Five ski runs vary in difficulty, height and steepness with the longest at 400 m (1,312 ft) with a 60 m (200 ft) drop for adrenaline-chasing snow junkies – the first indoor black run on the planet. A wide range of slopes make it suitable for skiers of every age and ability while snowboarders can also practice their tricks on a 90 m (300 ft)-long quarter pipe. No gear? No worries: Ski Dubai hires out ski gear and equipment and has a quad-chairlift and tow lift to ferry skiers across igloos, snowmen and sculpted ice to the piste.

📅 Year-round but most fun during Aug when the mercury can hit 45°C (113°F) outside!

ℹ Ski Dubai www.skidxb.com
Dubai Tourism www.dubaitourism.ae

Dubai's snow slopes are meticulously kept at -1°C (30°F)

1 Hatch Chile Festival

NORTH AMERICA

New Mexico, USA

Did you know that just a single fresh medium-sized green chilli boasts as much Vitamin C as six oranges? Or that of the 26 known species of chilli pepper all belong to the nightshade family? You'll learn all this – and more – at the Hatch Chile Festival, a two-day celebration of a fiery crop. As summer cools down, the people of Hatch feel the heat as Labor Day weekend heralds the arrival of 30,000 chilli-lovers – multiplying the population by 15 times overnight. After the crowning of the Chilli Queen, dozens of stalls serve up recipes rich in fresh and dried chillies while contests decide the chilli tossing champion.

📅 Weekend, early Sep

ℹ Hatch Chile Festival www.hatchchilefest.com
New Mexico Tourism www.newmexico.org

2 Moscow City Day

EUROPE

Russia

Thanks to Boris Yeltsin, Muscovites have a dedicated event at which to celebrate 900 years of glorious history. Introduced in 1986 by the Moscow City Committee, Moscow's City Day dominates the city over the first weekend in September. Festivities get underway with a patriotic Saturday procession that culminates in rousing speeches at the Kremlin. Then, it's time for frivolity as the weekend begins in earnest with street parties, fun fairs and music in every park and plaza washed down with copious slugs of vodka.

📅 2nd Sep

ℹ Russia Tourist Board www.visitrussia.org.uk

Old-fashioned street parties spread far and wide across the city

3 Cure Salée

AFRICA

Niger

Each year, Tuaregs and other Saharan nomads gather at the small oasis village of Ingall to lead their herds to nearby salt licks. Over the years, Cure Salée (meaning salt cure in French) has taken on a festival atmosphere that draws in nomadic groups with their vast herds of cattle. Ingall's mineral salt deposits rid livestock's digestive systems from parasites while festival-goers barter, socialise and arrange weddings in a colourful event of dance, music and camel racing.

📅 Sep 3rd

ℹ Niger Tourism www.niger-tourisme.com

4 Kashmir's Lakes

India – Pakistan

Readers are taken on a journey through India's Kashmir region in the early 20th century in Salman Rushdie's evocative first-person narrative Midnight's Children. Tales of lush landscapes, lavish colours and delectable aromas cast Rushdie more as a painter than a writer. Today, Kashmir still abounds in rich, vibrant colours – especially around its flora-rich lakes – where visitors can soak up the region's beauty from a 20-room palatial-style houseboat of intricately-carved wood on the waters of the peaceful Dal Lake.

📅 May – Sep

ℹ Kashmir Houseboats www.houseboatskashmir.com
Meena Houseboats www.meenahouseboats.com

Enjoy a leisurely passage across the peaceful lake amidst varicoloured flora

5 Braemar Gathering
| EUROPE

Scotland

There have been Gatherings of one sort or another at Braemar since the days of King Malcolm Canmore, 900 years ago. Always held on the first Saturday in September, the event is one of Scotland's oldest and biggest highland gatherings with a fiercely-fought programme of competitive events, including highland dancing, piping, tossing the caber, hammer throwing, putting the stone, long leap and tug of war.

This traditional celebration of Scottish sports boasts a scenic setting, just 13 km (8 miles) from Balmoral Castle at the gateway to Royal Deeside amidst wild deer and pheasant.

📅 First Saturday in Sep
❶ Braemar Gatering www.braemargathering.org
   Visit Scotland www.visitscotland.com

6 Surf the Severn Bore
| EUROPE

Gloucestershire, England

According to legend, the tidal bore (wave) on the River Severn's estuary denotes the mood of the goddess Sabrina who rides the wave in her chariot accompanied by dolphins and salmon, both species once common to the waterway. When calm, the river is small and unbroken, but when Sabrina is angry, the waters become turbulent and foaming as the bore rises up. These days, it is hardy local and international surfers who attempt to surf the wave for as long as possible, with rides of several hundred metres possible. If you're not up to surfing the wave, then chasing the Severn Bore along its 28 km (17 mile) course can be a thrilling experience too.

📅 2 per day for 130 days per year, depending on tides (but autumn or spring are best)
❶ Tidal Bore Research Society www.tidalbore.info

Hardy souls surf the River Severn tidal bore

7 Novel Madness Competition | NORTH AMERICA

Vancouver, Canada

Novel Madness draws hundreds of budding writers to Vancouver over the Labor Day weekend, with pens poised. The World's Most Notorious Literary Marathon sets would-be authors a tough challenge – to produce a masterwork of fiction in three short days. Since 1977, Novel Madness has been responsible for dozens of published novels, thousands of first drafts, countless good ideas and a reality TV series from a zillion crazed plotlines and coffee-stained pages.

📅 3-days, early Sep (Labor Day weekend)

ℹ Novel Madness www.3daynovel.com
   Vancouver Tourism www.tourismvancouver.com

8 Climbing Mt Kilimanjaro | AFRICA

Tanzania

Picking the best time to climb Mount Kilimanjaro can be the difference between seeing the summit and merely reaching it. At 5,893 m (19,336 ft), the snow-capped peak in Tanzania is Africa's highest with five different climatic zones and a half-dozen walkable trails to the top, including the popular Marangu. Mountain rainforests lead to scrub and alpine moorland before the ice fields of the summit. Keen to avoid the crowds and downpours? Then climb in September for cloud-free days and peaceful trails.

📅 Sep is best month

ℹ Tanzania Tourism tanzaniatouristboard.com
   National Parks of Tanzania www.tanzaniaparks.com

At 5,893 metres (19,336 feet) Mt Kilimanjaro spans five climate zones

9 Chinatown Autumn Festival

Singapore

In 1821, the first Chinese junk arrived from Xiamen to settle to the south of Singapore River. Using bullock-drawn drays, Chinatown slowly evolved into a fully-fledged community, known as Niu Che Shui (meaning Bullock Cart Water). Expect street calligraphy, tea ceremonies, medicine stalls, ginseng, bird cages, herb-sellers, fresh dim sum and shops selling rolls of Chinese silk, trinkets and necklaces of jade. September brings the city's Autumn Festival (celebrated on the 15th day of the eighth lunar month) when a spectacular 1,200 m (4,000 ft) illuminated dragon-shaped lantern adorns the riverbank together with hundreds of sizzling noodle and fried rice stalls.

23 Sep

🛈 www.visitsingapore.com

Browse tea shops, calligraphy stalls and herb-sellers in Chinatown

10 BodyGras

Nanaimo Harbour City, Canada

Since the caveman era, humans have daubed their bodies with colour. Today, a Canadian body-painting festival takes this ancient art to a whole new level. Using naked flesh as a canvass, 30 of the world's finest body artists come to Nanaimo's Harbour City for the three-day event started by professional airbrush artist Jeff King. After Friday workshops, and demos, the public can enter on Saturday to view the artists at work. Each 'exhibit' takes around six hours to complete with plenty of paint required in order to skirt Canada's indecency laws – models wear little else than the art itself. Every artistic scope is explored transforming models into wild animals, mythological creatures, mechanical contraptions and abstract concepts.

23 Weekend, early Sep

🛈 Body Gras www.canadianbodypaintingfestival.com

11 Hot Water Beach | AUSTRALIA/PACIFIC

Whitianga, New Zealand

Anyone arriving with a spade at low tide on Hot Water Beach is welcome to dig a hole and plonk themselves in for a soak in volcano-fed steaming tidal pools. Don't rely on a sandcastle scoop – you'll need a big garden shovel to excavate a pool with a decent depth. Then lie back and enjoy Pacific Ocean views, framed by tufted pohutukawa trees and a long shard of cliffs.

In Sep there's wildlife aplenty and fewer people about

Hot Water Beach Tourism www.hotwaterbeach.co.nz

Mercury Bay Touirsm www.mercurybay.co.nz

Bring a shovel to take full advantage of Hot Water Beach

12 Fall Colours | NORTH AMERICA

Vermont, USA

In early September, Vermont's crisp, green leaves transform to yellow-gold in the centre and north of the state. As the season progresses, a magical display of resplendent foliage forms a sharp contrast to the white clapboarded villages as thousands of visitors arrive. A variety of factors turn leaves golden brown and russet red from light level and temperature to soil conditions and rainfall. Colour changes tend to accelerate in late September to provide a vibrant array of crimson red, coppery yellows, russets, gold and bronze across the state until late October when the last lingering, bright maples are found in Vermont's lowland regions. Arrive in the second week in September to witness the first fiery flares of colour in Burke Mountain, Jay Peak, Mount Mansfield and Belvidere Mountain. Not is the air crisp and sunny but Vermont is almost entirely crowd-free, unlike the first two weekends of October – the busiest time for tourism in the year.

Vermont's seasonal progression in colour is spectacular

Early Sep – Late Oct (early Sep will beat the crowds)

Vermont Tourism www.vermontvacation.com

13 Ludlow Food Festival

EUROPE

England

For a small England-Wales border town, Ludlow boasts a large food tradition. Hundreds of organic farmers, cider and wine producers, independent cheese-makers, family-owned butchers and bakers take part in Ludlow's annual three-day Food & Drink festival. People visit from miles around to sample homemade sausages, brand new ales or enter a pudding competition in a region that boasts more Michelin-starred restaurants than any other place in the UK outside London. Try home-cured bacon, forest-reared venison, slow-rising breads and orchard jams in the magnificent grounds of Ludlow Castle.

📅 Mid Sept
ℹ️ Ludlow Tourist Bureau   www.ludlow.org.uk

14 Matchmaking

EUROPE

Lisdoonvarna, Co Clare, Ireland

Until 150 years ago the small town of Lisdoonvarna in Ireland's County Clare was a simple spa resort, renowned for its bubbling mineral-rich springs. Due to the popularity of the curative waters and the huge numbers they attracted, the town developed a reputation for romantic coupling. Singletons from the farming community began to arrive in their droves during September, once the harvest was safely in. By the 1920s, matchmaking was very much in vogue with visitors arriving to 'take the waters'. Today, the tradition continues and attracts single people from all over the world, led by two official Country Clare Matchmakers – Mr Willie Daly who runs the riding centre outside Ennistymon and Mr James White, hotelier and proprietor of the Lisdoonvarna Imperial Hotel. A Matchmaker's role involves pairing couples and orchestrating the annual festival.

For most of September and early October the merriment begins daily at 12 noon with free-flowing drink, Irish folk music and jigs. Set dancing displays, horse racing, Irish bands and traditional foods are central to the festival with fun and frolics (known as the "craic" in Irish) that continue into the early hours.

After a few hours sleep and a hearty Irish breakfast the revelling begins all over again – often after a glass of spa water by way of 'recovery'. One of the most popular events of the festival is the Speed Dating Weekend, allowing each singleton the opportunity to enjoy 50 three-minute dates. Men rotate, ladies remain seated and a clanging bell signifies it is time to move on. Participants receive a list of successful dates the following day – and so the fun begins. As a festival finale, 'Mr Lisdoonvarna' and the 'Queen of the Burren' competition results in the crowning of the event's most eligible lady and gentleman – a coveted title sought by upward of 40,000 romantic hopefuls.

📅 Mid-Sep – mid-Oct
ℹ️ MatchMaker Ireland   www.matchmakerireland.com
Ireland Tourism   www.discoverireland.com

15 Independence Day

Dolores Hidalgo, Mexico

At midnight on 15th September, the Mexican town of Dolores Hidalgo commemorates the impassioned speech of Padre Miguel Hidalgo y Costilla on the same night in 1810 – prompting the fight for independence against Spain. On this day only, the church bells ring as people pay homage to Miguel Hidalgo's statue in the plaza. Mexican flags, banners, and streamers in red, white, and green adorn buildings and cars as dawn-to-dusk drinking, dancing and fireworks fill the streets for two days.

📅 15th Sep (plus eve of 14th)

ℹ️ Mexico Tourism www.visitmexico.com

Dolores Hidalgo www.doloreshidalgo.gob.mx

16 Muriwai Beach Gannet Colony

Auckland, New Zealand

Rugged, windswept coastal rocks, crashing surf and rolling black-sand dunes characterize Auckland's Muriwai Beach. Protected as Muriwai Regional Park since 1969, the stretch from Maori Bay includes one of three mainland gannet colonies in New Zealand. Around 2,400 feisty gannets reside in pairs on the beach from mid-September to February. An elegant looking bird, the Australasian gannet is distinctive for its white body, striking black wing tips and yellow head. Gannets take between three to seven years to reach maturity, laying one chalky blue egg. Chicks hatch in November, embarking on a migration to Australia at 15 weeks old before returning to the colony at Muriwai Beach to breed.

📅 Mid – Sep to Feb

ℹ️ New Zealand Tourism www.newzealand.com

Muriwai Around 2,400 feisty gannets reside in pairs on Muriwai Beach

September

17 Last Night of the Proms

London, England

For over a century, since 1895, the BBC Prom Season has delighted London's concert goers with a rousing classical music extravaganza of more than 70 concerts over 58 days, allowing music fans to enjoy dozens of works from some of history's greatest composers. In addition to such luminaries as Elgar, Vivaldi and Beethoven you'll also find the innovative, untested and contemporary. In past years, The Proms has showcased British film scores and unknown homespun composers to provide an eclectic mix of daring performances – earning a much-deserved reputation as a not-to-be-missed musical jamboree of distinction that champions new music, composers and artists.

Each annual Proms Season invites many hundreds of musicians and singers from a wide variety of musical disciplines to concerts at the Royal Albert Hall.

However, the highlight of the festival is arguably the Last Night of the Proms – a rowdy celebration of over a million people swishing Union Jacks and blowing whistles in patriotic merriment. A perennially popular, affair, the Last Night at the Proms offers a chance to revel in a musical tradition of considerable pomp, pageantry and circumstance – an exhilarating, fun-filled finale conducted with energetic aplomb.

📅 Last night of a 2 month festival, Sep
ℹ️ BBC Proms www.bbc.co.uk/proms

Over 70 concerts in around 60 days culminates in a rousing classical music extravaganza

18 Eid ul-Fitr

Dubai

Muslims all over the world anticipate Eid ul-Fitr (Id-Ul-Fitr) with awe and pleasure after 30 days of self discipline and sacrifice. The sight of a crescent moon marks the end of Ramadan, the Islamic holy month of fasting. Three days of celebration ensue as Shawwal (the tenth month in the Islamic calendar) begins. Airports and border crossings in UAE are busy at this joyous time as people visit family and friends. Foreigners are often welcomed to join Eid festivities in Dubai or other cosmopolitan emirates and should bid the traditional Arabic greeting "Eid Mubarak! Allah yubaarak feek" ("Blessed Eid! May Allah bless it for you also!") or "Ayaamak Saeeda" when entering a home for coffee and snacks of dates and nuts.

📅 End of Ramadan

ℹ️ Dubai Tourism www.dubaitourism.ae

19 Surfing Eisbach (Ice Creek)

Munich, Germany

If surfing in Germany sounds about as plausible as snowboarding in the Sahara, think again. Despite very little sun and no beach, land-locked Munich is a cult surfing Mecca, boasting a boarding scene that has been Germany's best-kept secret since the 1970s. Nobody knows who laid the three rows of concrete blocks along the canal bottom to reduce the flow of water surging up from underground. This underwater ridge has been enhanced with some wooden boards wedged into the canal by local surfers. The result is a fast but surfable standing wave of wildly gushing rapids that has created a year-round surf spot. It may not be Malibu Beach – but there's not a shark in sight.

Munich's river surfing is centred on the Eisbach (or "Ice Creek") where two underground canals converge under the Prinzregentenstrasse Bridge. Balance is a key focus as is avoiding injury from the concrete blocks. Once in the water, a complex curl is tricky to master as all the energy is at the front. Much like a wind-tunnel on turbo, the powerful oncoming current pushes backwards - threatening the humiliation of being dumped down-water.

No sharks in sight: Ice creek's surfable standing wave

📅 Jun – early Oct, the water is warm enough to surf without shivering, though a wetsuit is still a must

ℹ️ Munich Tourist Office www.munich-tourist.de

20 Gai Jatra (Cow Festival) | ASIA

Kathmandu, Nepal

Nepal's Gai Jatra (Cow Festival) mixes satire with age-old tradition each August-September. As a memorial to newly-dead relatives, boys in cow-like attire parade through the streets of Kathmandu with a live cow on a rope, a ritual tinged with sadness but still subject to joking around. Laughter is a major part of the purging process for the bereaved, according to Nepalese tradition, with Gai Jatra a stepping-stone to accepting death as a part of life.

📅 Aug - Sep

ℹ️ Visit Nepal www.visitnepal.com

Gai Jatra uses humour in a joyous celebration of the dearly departed

21 Hermanus Whale Festival | AFRICA

South Africa

Positive eco-messages and a joyous celebration of spring combine at South Africa's annual Hermanus Whale Festival, held in honour of the arrival of the Southern Right whales to the waters of Walker Bay. Whale watching, shark cage diving, birding, hikes and kayak trips are just some of the highlights at this family-orientated eco-fest. As the nation's only Enviro-Arts shindig, the festival attracts thousands of visitors to the sleepy coastal resort of Hermanus for a mix of African music, comedy acts and handicrafts in conjunction with marine conservation bodies, green artisans and sustainable living campaigners.

📅 4 days late Sep

ℹ️ Hermanus Whale Festival www.whalefestival.co.za

Honouring the arrival of migratory whales with a 4 day eco-fest

22 Open House

London, England

Every September, Londoners are encouraged to re-examine their city during an 'Open House' weekend. In an event designed to open the debate about how architecture affects daily lives, over 700 buildings in England's buzzing capital throw open their doors to the public. Thousands of people enjoy walks around different styles of built environment, talks about design and taking advantage of a chance to get inside some of the iconic buildings that make up the city's skyline.

📅 2 days, end of Sep
ℹ️ Open House www.openhouse.org.uk
   London Tourist Board www.visitlondon.com

23 Singing Sands

Gobi Desert, Mongolia

The Khongory Els (meaning 'Singing Sands' on account of the noise made by the wind as passes across the dunes, causing the rounded grains to rub against each other) extends for 185 km (115 miles) across the southern Gobi Desert between Mounts Sevrei and Zuulun. Descriptions of the sand's musical qualities range from a gentle, low, deep hum to a high pitched operatic-style shriek and crescendo-roar with the outer layer of undulating dunes acting as a giant amplifier. Songs can last for a few seconds or continue for minutes if not hours. To enjoy the eerie wind-blown melodies of Kongory Els – and not get toasted by searing heat – visit the Gobi Desert September to October. From late October, the climate is unpredictable and prone to extremes, including sudden snowstorms and extreme cold. Locals consider April and May the worst-weather months.

📅 Sep – Oct
ℹ️ Mongolia Tourism www.mongoliatourism.gov.mn

An eerie wind-blown melody fills the dunes of the Gobi desert

24 Tiger Fish Fishing | AFRICA

Lake Kariba, Zambia

Home to hard-fighting tiger fish up to 13.5 kg (30 lbs) in weight, Lake Kariba is a serious sport angler's paradise. Attracting fishermen from all over the world, this Zambezi reservoir offers a rare opportunity to hunt the elusive, ultra-aggressive tiger fish in waters the size of an inland sea. Expect to see grazing buffalo herds on the banks of the lake together with elephant, rhino, hippo, crocodile and other big game. Waters are clean and calm from early to mid-September, when anglers are drawn to the lake, although Lake Kariba is fishable year-round.

23 Clear and calm waters in mid-Sept

ⓘ Zambia Tourism www.zambiatourism.com

25 Galway Oyster Festival | EUROPE

Ireland

For over half a century, thousands of people have gathered at Ireland's world-renowned four-day oyster festival to celebrate the nation's seafood tradition with plenty of old-fashioned Irish music and the best Guinness in town. Marking the start of the oyster season, the Galway International Oyster Festival kicks off with an Oyster Opening Contest on the Thursday evening, before an ultra-swish ticket-only Mardis Gras event on Friday night. The newly crowned Pearl (Oyster Queen) presents the season's first oyster to Galway's Mayor on Saturday – a tradition since 1954 – amidst parades, a street carnival and much merriment. On Sunday, a farewell gala dinner and closing party brings more Oyster-themed delights.

23 4 days, late Sep

ⓘ Galway International Oyster Festival
www.galwayoysterfest.com

Marking the start of the oyster season with food, drink and song

26 Road Kill Cook Off

Marlington, USA

Fancy a serving of sweet 'n' sour squirrel, deep-fried possum, teriyaki deer or bear stew? Then head to Marlington for their annual Road Kill Cook Off where the motto is "You kill it, we grill it!" One of West Virginia's most unpredictable food festivals, Road Kill Cook Off celebrates state laws allowing residents to eat animals killed on the road. Expect to find the

locals scraping away at the asphalt from early morning for this wacky culinary event – the menu is whatever's been mowed down.

📅 Last Saturday in Sep

ℹ️ pccocwv.com/festival.htm

27 Finding of the True Cross (Meskel)

Ethiopia

The first big festival of the Ethiopian religious calendar commemorates the finding of the true cross by St Helena in the fourth century AD. Today this great religious feast is fused with older, traditional rites in honour of the return of sunshine after the gloom of the rainy season – just as the bright yellow Meskel daisy reaches full bloom. A riot of colour, hope and joy, the Meskel Festival is celebrated with bonfires, parties, chanting, flame-lit torch parades and public celebrations. Tradition dictates that people return to the bonfire the following morning to etch the sign of the cross on their foreheads with ash. St Helena is said to have given fragments of Christ's cross to all the churches of the world – the Ethiopian Church still claims to have theirs in the remote monastery of Gishan Mariam.

📅 Late Sep

ℹ️ Ethiopia Tourism www.tourismethiopia.org

Bonfires, chanting and flame-lit parades characterize Meskel

28 Ibiza Closing Parties

Spain

As the pumping heat of the peak season sun shows signs of weakening, Ibiza's banging party scene gets ready to spin its final groove. Only the die-hards plan ahead for the party finale, packing fancy dress gear along with their skimpy clubbing garb and texting home to lure clubbing pals back for the last hurrah. Even Europe's top-name DJs fly in to leave their mark on the decks at the end of Ibiza's season. From afternoon dance sets on the sun terrace and spin-masters dropping ace high-energy mixes to midnight retro trance with an 'underground' feel – it's all got a place in Ibiza's big adios as Amnesia, Zoo and Space get the crowds sweaty for one last night of vibes.

🗓 Last week in Sep

ℹ Ibiza Spotlight Clubbing Guide www.ibiza-spotlight.com
Balearic Island Tourism www.illesbalears.es

Club-goers worldwide head to Ibiza for its pumping 'closing parties'

29 Vegetarian Festival

Phuket, Thailand

Not for the squeamish, Thailand's 10-day Vegetarian Festival features some truly bizarre facial piercings in a ritual that traces its roots back to the early 1800s. Expect grotesquely misshapen tongues, speared cheeks and oddball piercings in other parts of the body at an event first staged to ward off evil spirits and bring good fortune. Today, the people of Phuket Island uphold this painful-looking tradition while refraining from all impure thoughts and deeds. Eating meat, drinking alcohol, engaging in sex, quarrelling, telling lies, fighting and killing are all off the menu.

🗓 End of Sep - early Oct

ℹ Thailand Tourism www.tourismthailand.org

Gruesome facial piercings are all the rage at Phuket's Vegetarian Festival

30 Oktoberfest

Munich, Germany

The Oktoberfest in Munich runs for a full 16 days from late-September to early-October and attracts over six-million people to the Bavarian capital. Since 1818, beers served at the event (Oktoberfestbiers) have represented the half-dozen main breweries of Bavaria: Spaten, Löwenbräu, Augustiner, Hofbräu, Hacker-Pschorr and Paulaner. Traditionally these were malty, dark beers, although Oktoberfest is now renowned for its lagers at around five-six per cent strength, ranging in colour from golden blonde to deep amber. On the first day of the festival, hundreds of thousands of beer drinkers converge on the site at noon – with one thing on their minds. Many have claimed their seats at breakfast time but are resigned to waiting until the clock strikes 12, when the city's mayor taps the first keg of Oktoberfest beer followed by a "Böllerschießen" (a 12-gun canon salute) in front of the Bavaria statue. Then, and only then, can the thirst-quenching commence.

The first Oktoberfest was held in the winter of 1810 in honour of the Bavarian Crown Prince Ludwig's marriage to Princess Therese von Sachsen-Hildburghausen. In the years that followed, the celebrations gradually grew more extensive and were moved to September to allow for better weather. In warmer evenings, beer drinkers began the tradition of sitting outside the tents at long tables. Highlights include the lederhosen-clad Oktoberfest Costume and Riflemen's Parade on the first Wiesn Sunday and the grand ceremony of the Oktoberfest Landlords and Breweries. Several tons of traditional Bavarian fare are consumed during the festival, including enough Schweinsbraten (roast pork), Würstel (sausage) and Knödeln (potato or bread dumplings) to sink a ship. Over $US 126 million (95 million Euro) is spent during the festival – almost all of it on beer.

Over 6 million beer-lovers descend on Munich for the Oktoberfest

📅 16 days, late-Sep – early-Oct
ℹ️ Oktoberfest www.oktoberfest.de
   Munich Tourist www.munich-tourist.de

Diwali at the Golden Temple, Amritsar, India

Climb Ancient Mauna Kea | NORTH AMERICA

Hawaii, USA

Meaning "White Mountain" in Hawaiian, Mauna Kea began forming about one million years ago and is distinctive for its snow-capped winter peaks and 11 m (36 ft) permafrost. A signed path tortuously stumbles its way up the ultra-steep south side to the Visitor Information Station at about 2,834 m (9297 ft) before an 8 km (5 mile) stretch to the crater's rim. Home to a state-of-the-art observatory, the distant glow of the Kilauea Volcano adds an ethereal ambience to this sacred site for star-gazing where eye-popping night views in an alpine setting have an otherworldly feel.

📅 Dry season (Apr – end of Oct)
ℹ Hawaii Tourism www.hawaii-tourism.co.uk

Clad in 11 metres (36 ft) of permafrost Hawaii's Mauna Kea has an alpine feel

Plastic Duck Race | EUROPE

Tübingen, Germany

On your marks, get set, quack! Up to 7,000 plastic yellow ducks make a break for it on open water in Germany each October. Held annually, the Tübinger Duck Race owes more to river tides than racing skill but that doesn't stop thousands of onlookers from yelling advice as owners attempt to chivvy their coot along. At 2pm a starting gun fires at Alleenbrücke, but arrive an hour earlier to rent a duck with winning pedigree.

📅 Oct
ℹ Tübinger Duck Race www.tuebinger-entenrennen.de

More than 7,000 plastic ducks in Germany's annual river coot race

3 Mt Rushmore Marathon | NORTH AMERICA

USA

As the trees change colour the Mount Rushmore Marathon course becomes a stunning array of swirling copper, crimson and bronze. Winding through the Black Hills of South Dakota, Mt. Rushmore National Memorial, and Crazy Horse Memorial to the early 19th-century train station in Downtown Hill City – with full marathon and half-marathon routes available for competitors that range from fun-run plodders to the speedy super-fit.

📅 Sunday, early Oct

ℹ️ Mt Rushmore Marathon www.mountrushmoremarathon.com

4 Diwali at the Golden Temple | ASIA

Amritsar, India

Celebrated by Hindus, Jains and Sikhs all over the world, Diwali is known as the festival of light. Lamps and candles are lit as a symbol of hope for humanity as families and friends gather to celebrate the triumph of good over evil. Amritsar's Diwali attracts thousands of devotees to the holy city's Golden Temple. Crowds pay obeisance at the shrine as the sky fills with a feast of fireworks and illuminations.

📅 Spread across 5 days, at the new moon, Oct – Nov

ℹ️ India Tourism www.incredibleindia.org

Thousands of devotees head for Amritsar's holy Golden Temple

5 Navaratri | ASIA

Kuala Lumpur, Malaysia

Meaning "nine nights," the festival of Navarathiri commemorates the Goddess Durga's lengthy fight with the demonic Asura – an important triumph of good over evil. Considered the personification of courage, strength, and power, Durga is honoured for her admirable values during a festival blessed with prayers and dance. In Kuala Lumpur, nine dance organizations take part in the nine-day Navarathiri at the Asthana Arts Central Market in a vibrant display of exotic Indian classical dance traditions.

📅 9 days, early – mid Oct

ℹ️ Malaysian Tourist Office www.tourismmalaysia.gov.my

6 The River of Raptors

| NORTH AMERICA

Veracruz, Mexico

Every autumn, on Mexico's eastern coast around five million birds of prey embark on the world's largest and most spectacular raptor migration. The town of Cardel, an hour from the city of Veracruz, allows an unsurpassed view of the raptors as they fly south for the winter – a gap between the eastern Sierra Madres and the Gulf of Mexico extends all the way to northern Canada, funnelling virtually all the raptors through a narrow chute. Birds leave at around 10 am as the sun begins to heat the earth, rising to an updraft with apparent ease. Hundreds or thousands of birds pass overhead in a dramatic formation of broad-winged, soaring hawks and vultures.

📅 Migration from Aug – Nov

ℹ Mexico Tourism www.visitmexico.com

Over 5 million birds of prey fly south during the raptor migration

7 Buffalo Racing

| ASIA

Vihear Suor, Cambodia

Around 75 years ago, the farmers of Vihear Suor were faced with devastation when their water buffalo herds grew ill from a mystery disease. Water buffalo are vital to rural Cambodians as they provide the muscle to plough fields together with the transport to haul crops to market. The villagers prayed to a spirit to help save their animals and pledged to show their gratitude by holding a buffalo race each year on the last day of P'chum Ben - Cambodia's festival for dead ancestors. Today, thousands converge on the village 50 km (31 miles) northeast of Phnom Penh. After paying their respects to the Neakta Preah Srok pagoda spirit, each buffalo owner parades his charge proudly throughout the village. As promised, Vihear Suor village stages the water buffalo races to mark the final day of P'chum Ben's festivities, draping their buffalo in colourful fabric. A number of highly-competitive races pit buffalos against each other, spurred on by bareback riders on a route of hard-packed, dry mud. Fancy dress contests and a Miss Farmer Pageant offer some light-hearted relief together with some mock races for children. After the ceremony, the buffaloes are sold to the highest bidder before a traditional wrestling match caps off the festival amidst great cheering and feasting.

📅 Mid Oct

ℹ Cambodia Tourism www.tourismcambodia.com

8 Círio De Nazaré (Amazon Festival) | SOUTH AMERICA

Belém, Brazil

Dubbed 'The Lungs of the Earth', the Amazon region stretches over eight countries in South America covering an area not much smaller than Australia or the 48 contiguous United States. In celebration of this wonderful expanse, the port town of Belém in Brazil stages the Círio De Nazaré, the largest annual festival along this immense inky-green river, on the second weekend in October. Expect hundreds of decorated boats and a procession centred on the effigy of the Virgin of Nazaré to the Basílica de Nazaré.

📅 2nd weekend of Oct

ℹ Cirio de Nazare www.ciriodenazare.com.br

9 Horseback Archery | ASIA

Ana-hachimangu Shrine, Tokyo, Japan

Since the Heian period (AD794-1191) the ceremonial art of shooting whistling arrows at stationary targets from the back of a galloping horse has been a martial equine art in the Japanese warrior tradition. Today, the practice of yabusame is almost exclusively considered a religious rite with the shooting of three targets used as a divination for the year's harvest.

Near to the resplendent Ana-hachimangu Shrine in Tokyo, the annual Ana-hachimangu Yabusame showcases the ancient art of Japanese horseback archery with ancient rituals, costumes and deities.

📅 Oct 9th

ℹ Japan National Tourist Office www.jnto.go.jp

Witness the galloping horses and martial equine art in the Japanese warrior tradition

10 Conker Championship | EUROPE

Ashton, England

On the second Sunday in October the village of Ashton welcomes thousands to a spectacle involving a conker (a horse chestnut) and 30 cm (12 in) of string. First staged in 1965, the World Conker Championships now attracts conker nuts from as far afield as Mexico, Australia and Asia. Fruits of the chestnut tree develop in prickly cases but ripen in September and October – the conker 'season'. Competitors battle for glory on the village green. Winners are crowned on a Conker Throne.

⊠ 2nd Sunday in Oct

❶ World Conker Championship
www.worldconkerchampionships.com

Players from around the globe compete for the Conker Throne

12 Saijo Sake Festival | ASIA

Hiroshima, Japan

Two thousand years ago, the Japanese believed that sake bestowed power from the gods. At Saijo's Sake Festival, it's easy to believe in super-human forces as hundreds of grinning drinkers make the most of refill cups. As the home of eight old and prestigious breweries, Saijo is at the forefront of Japan's ancient art of sake-making with the start of the winter brewing season heralded at the sake festival. Cold weather slows down fermentation to create a tarter, more acidic flavour. The finest winter-brewed sake boasts a rice aroma and a fresh-fruit taste that dances on the tongue. Sake is 16 percent alcohol – with a potent kick that goes straight to the head and renders the drinker distinctly worse for wear the following morning.

⊠ Weekend mid Oct

❶ Hiroshima Tourism www.hcvb.city.hiroshima.jp
Japan National Tourist Office www.jnto.go.jp

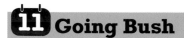

11 Going Bush

AUSTRALIA/PACIFIC

Lichfield National Park, Australia

Popularized by reality TV, the Australian bush has provided its people with a giant store-cupboard for centuries. What's on the bush tucker 'menu' depends on the season. Hunters and gatherers traditionally snared toads, snakes, lizards and possums for diet staples with nyilli nyilli (bush bubblegum), bardi grubs, berries and nuts as snacks. Take a Bush Tucker hike in Litchfield National Park, April to October.

📅 Apr – Oct

ℹ Northern Territory National Parks www.nt.gov.au
Litchfield National Park Tours www.litchfieldnationalpark.com

13 Kashgar Sunday Market

ASIA

Xingxiang, China

Once the last outfitting station on the centuries-old Silk Road, Kashgar Market seems stuck in a time warp each Sunday when entire families and communities gather at one of the world's liveliest bazaars. A mesmerizing Muslim city at the westernmost frontier of China, Kashgar boasts considerable verve and spirit born out of a fusion of cultural influences from neighbouring Central Asian countries. Vast pens of sheep, camels, carts laden with goats and caged birds of every description provide a wall of sound. A rainbow of spices spill into the dust while crowds haggle over textiles, trinkets, flatbreads, and slabs of mutton in a market tradition unchanged by history – or a recent lick of paint.

📅 Every Sunday. Oct offers relief from high summer temperatures

ℹ China National Tourist Office www.cnto.org

14 Dive the Blue Lagoon

EUROPE

Silfra, Iceland

Silfra has been dubbed the "coolest place to dive on Earth" – and with water temperatures at around 2°C this is pretty spot-on. Mist-shrouded glacial waters and ancient lava beds typify the rugged terrain, just 40-minutes drive from Reykjavik's urban sprawl, but a world away. Born out of a crevice created by a geological shift that divides the European and American continental plates, Silfra's underwater chasm is expanding by around 2 cm (1 in) each year. Filled with melt water from the icecaps of the Hofsjokull Mountains the porous volcanic rock acts as a filter. So dramatic is the clarity that waters shimmer and glitter like cut-class - hence the name "Silver Lady" (or Silfra in Icelandic). Visibility up to 100 m (328 ft) is common. Nature stands little chance of supporting much aquatic life at such low temperatures so the waters boast a space-like dreaminess with shafts of sunlight in autumn adding an intergalactic quality as you dive into its icy depths.

📅 Year-round (though it's more beautiful when the sun shines)

ℹ Scuba Iceland www.scubaiceland.com
Thingvellir National Park www.thingvellir.is

15 Javanese Apothecary

Bali, Indonesia

Amongst ancient Javanese artifacts the Seger Waras Spa (meaning fresh and healthy) pays homage to Eastern health philosophies. Nuts, flowers and spices are picked daily from aromatic gardens, then ground into pastes, powders and potions and scented using frangipani, tropical magnolia, rose, jasmine and ylang-ylang. Step across bridged lotus pools and spurting fountains to a Balinese pavilion studded with carved Garudas and Boma Heads (mythological guardians) for a sensual touch-therapy using coconut oil and wave-smoothed energy stones – to the plink-plonk lulling rhythms of the gamelan.

23 Apr – Oct (dry season)

ⓘ Waroeng Djamoe Spa at The Tugu www.tuguhotels.com
Indonesian Tourist Office www.my-indonesia.info

Pick herbs, spices, nuts and blooms from an all-natural apothecary

16 Hustle and Salsa Festival

Puerto Rico, USA

Thousands of snake-hipped sassy, salsa movers head to Puerto Rico for the three-day annual Hustle and Salsa Festival in the self-proclaimed "Salsa Capital of the World". Alongside workshops, displays, live music and fiercely-fought salsa competitions the Festival is renowned for its wild, sweaty salsa parties – a gathering point for salseros and mambo queens from all over the world. Local bars stay open late, while Puerto Rico's clubs and DJs do their best to outshine each other – providing a great opportunity to hang out with world-class movers.

23 3 days, Oct

ⓘ Puerto Rico Tourism www.gotopuertorico.com

17 Shark Alley

Gansbaai, South Africa

The name 'Shark Alley' says it all – a stretch of water just half-hour off the South African mainland rich in Mother Nature's most fearsome underwater killing machines. As skilled predators, great whites patrol the deeper water as well as the edges of the kelp fields in the area around Gansbaai – the 'Great White Shark Diving Capital of the World'. Shark Alley is best visited in winter (May to October) when the sharks are in a high state of excitement due to a ready supply of seal pups, and cage-diving boats offer tourists a chance to slip on a wetsuit and take a closer look – often eyeball to-eyeball through 12 mm (0.5 in) of galvanized steel mesh.

📅 May – Oct
ℹ️ South Africa Tourism www.southafrica.net
Great White Shark Diving www.greatwhitesharkdiving.co.za
White Shark Diving www.white-shark-diving.com

Come eye-ball to eye-ball with the skillful underwater killing machines

18 Star-gazing at Sedona

Arizona, USA

Strict ordinances on light pollution ensure the dark skies over Sedona are ideal for star-gazing – or spotting UFOs – 100 have been sighted since 1977. Sedona boasts some of the clearest skies in North America. Dozens of professional astronomers offer guided cosmic journeys using powerful Dobsonian telescopes to pinpoint elusive constellations, spiral galaxies, the rings of Saturn, meteor showers, comets, Mars and star clusters.

📅 Oct (when the temperatures begin to cool off)
ℹ️ Arizona Tourism www.arizonaguide.com
Sirus Lookers (Astronomy Cub) www.siriuslookers.org
Department of Astronomy www.as.arizona.edu

19 Island Food Secrets | SOUTH AMERICA

Isla Colon, Panama

Home to around 40 ethnicities, Isla Colon is a melting pot of food influences, from the former banana trade workers in the Afro-Caribbean and Panama's nine indigenous tribes to the culinary sway of its neighbours Costa Rica and Colombia. In the quieter months of the off-peak tourist season (June to October), Gustavo Delano Smith, a big, cuddly bear of a man, passes on the island's kitchen secrets to food-loving tourists, from market tours and fish buying to whipping up dishes of maize, yucca, plantain, shrimp, lobster and octopus in old oil cans on the beach.

23 Jun – Oct (before the crowds arrive)

ℹ Bocas del Toro Tourism www.bocas.com

Savour a fresh mix of Latino-Caribbean flavours

20 Fantasy Fest | NORTH AMERICA

Florida, USA

For over a quarter of a century Key West has been hijacked by this exuberant 10-day costumed soiree – and today it rivals New Orleans' Mardi Gras in the number of out-of-towners it attracts. Over 100,000 partygoers (and counting) descend on neon-lit Duval Street in a riotous explosion of colour that triples the island's resident population overnight. Fantasy Fest mixes cutesy parades with glitzy masquerade balls, satirical shows and torch-lit cavalcades. Crowds of costume-clad face-painted revellers fill the streets, waving tinsel and fairy-lights for extra pizzazz. Bejewelled merrymakers in feathered rhinestone-studded garb wiggle and giggle in ritzy heels or sequin-covered roller-skates – determined to give it their all with over $US 10,000 in prizes up for grabs. On family-orientated Children's Day, thousands of kids in day-glow spandex juggle with paint bombs and dance with pixies, surrounded by candy stalls, street musicians, fire-eaters and clowns on stilts. Other oddball events include a Pet Fancy Dress Parade complete with an owner's look-a-like category – a real hoot when entrants include a pot-bellied pig and shrimps. A Royal Coronation Ball is a tongue-in-cheek highlight that culminates in the Monarchy of Masked Mayhem being crowned – an ultra-camp zenith to Key West's fun-filled frolics.

23 7 days, mid-Oct (main parade over a weekend)

ℹ Fantasy Fest www.fantasyfest.net

Anything goes at Key West's tongue-in-cheek Fantasy Fest

21 Gathering of the Elephants | ASIA

Minneriya Tank, Sri Lanka

Sri Lanka's famous Elephant Gathering takes place in the 8,890-hectare (22,000 acre) Minneriya National Park. During the dry season (July to October), when forest waterholes have vaporized into cracked patches of earth, a reservoir built in 3rd century AD by King Mahasena attracts herds of elephants in search of wet ground. After grazing on lush grasses, they frolic and bathe in the shallow waters alongside flocks of cormorants and painted storks.

📅 Jul – Oct (dry season)
ℹ Sri Lanka Tourism www.srilankatourism.org

Hundreds of elephants gather at the reservoir

22 Suriname Jazz Festival | AFRICA

Paramaribo, Suriname

Suriname's 4-day jazz explosion dominates the city of Paramaribo's bars, cafes and outdoor venues throughout the end of October. This seasonal highlight for music lovers may boast an annual theme – but that's where the format ends. Dozens of acts and artists from all over the region tease the audience with a delightful mix of styles – including Paramaribo's distinctive Wild Coast Sound, a delicious fusion of Samba and Jazz.

📅 Weekend, end of Oct
ℹ Suriname Jazz Festival www.surinamejazzfestival.com

23 Red Crab Migration | AUSTRALIA/PACIFIC

Christmas Island

Crabs get everywhere on Christmas Island – not only do they form great moving carpets on the beach but they scuttle through monsoon forest, edge across main roads, forage in private gardens and even hide in hotel closets. In Flying Fish Cove, the island's biggest concentration of crabs outnumbers its local population by at least 5,000-to-1 in a nation described as the "kingdom of crabs" by Sir David Attenborough. Home to some 14 species of land crab, of which the crimson-and-black coloured species is the most obvious, Christmas Island's 50-million crustacean inhabitants begin their annual migration at the start of the wet season, around October or November. As the rains start to fall, the crabs pick their way out of the forested interior with startling synchronicity, heading towards the sea to breed and lay their eggs.

Adult crabs can measure up to 116 mm (4½ in) in width at sexual maturity which, at around five years old, is when they follow a migratory urge. A lunar rhythm impacts the precise timing of migration to ensure the release of eggs coincides with turn of the tide (when difference between high and low tide is least). Everyday life on Christmas Island (population 1,350) adapts quickly to this mammoth migratory advance as plastic barriers are erected to herd the crabs into special underground tunnels

beneath major routes and some roads are closed. To witness the relentless journeying of the crabs to the shore, head to viewing spots at Drumsite, Flying Fish Cove, Ethel Beach and Greta Beach where onlookers struggle to absorb the sheer scale of this mammoth phenomenon. Hailed the "Galapagos of the Indian Ocean", two thirds of Christmas Island is a national park with the crab migration attracting around 1,500 visitors a year. The sound of millions of legs scuttling through the rainforest's dry leaf litter sounds like a sustained downpour as every centimetre of the island is transformed into a rippling scarlet sea.

23 Oct – Nov

ⓘ Christmas Island www.christmas.net.au

Moving carpets of migratory crabs dominate Christmas Island's streets

24 Rafting the Rio Chiriquí | SOUTH AMERICA

Panama

October to November mark the final throws of Panama's rainy season when Chiriquí's rapids are at their wildest and water levels are high. Chiriquí Viejo snakes for 128 km (80 miles) from Cerro Picacho to the town of Cerro Punta. From the Highlands, nourished by icy torrents, it crashes down the craggy slopes to emerge as a gushing rock-strewn fast-flowing river at the Volcan plains. Wide, choppy and prone to powerful surges, the Chiriquí Viejo is fast-emerging as one of Central America's most exhilarating white water rafting hotspots, offering

Class II-Class V rapids characterized by spectacular waterfalls and canyons. Chiriquí's turbulent frothing stretches offer average drops of 120-130 metres per kilometer amidst fearsome boulders. On calmer stretches, rafters can paddle past egrets, kingfishers, cormorants, blackbirds and iguana while vultures hover effortlessly overhead.

📅 Year-round, but the waters are quiet Oct – early Dec
ℹ️ Panama Rafting www.panama-rafting.com
    Panama Institute of Tourism www.visitpanama.com

25 Hawaiki Nui Va'a Canoe Race | AUSTRALIA/PACIFIC

Huahine-Bora Bora, Tahiti

Hundreds of six-man traditional Polynesian canoes compete in the Hawaiki Nui Va'a Race in October each year– a gruelling event that tests paddling skills and stamina over three tough days. On days one and two speed and power are crucial with the third day culminating in a demanding 52 km (32 mile) slog. Canoeists are cheered to the finishing line to be met

by the sound of drums and traditional singing in what surely must be the the largest and longest open ocean outrigger canoe event in the world.

📅 3 days, Oct
ℹ️ Tahiti Tourism www.tahiti-tourisme.com

26 Angam Day | AUSTRLIA/PACIFIC

Naura

In the 1920s, a serious 'flu epidemic wiped out a third of the tiny Pacific island of Nauru's population. Survivors were severely weakened by the illness prompting wide-spread fear that the community would die-out. It took 12 years for the population to reach full strength again – but on the 26th October, the 1,500th Nauruan (a baby girl called Eidaruwo)

was born. Today, Angam Day (Day of Fulfilment) commemorates the occasion as a joyous public holiday in recognition of the people of Nauru's determination to survive in the face of adversity.

📅 Oct 26th
ℹ️ www.discovernauru.com

27 Outdoor BBQ, Mercado del Puerto | SOUTH AMERICA

Montevideo, Uraguay

Visitors who arrive in Uruguay having missed the
gluttonous food-filled summer feasts can make up
for time at Montevideo's historic Mercado del
Puerto – dubbed 'Meat Heaven'. Dozens of wood-
fired ovens, open pits and charcoal-fired grills
smoke, sizzle and hiss in dozens of steak joints and
meat grills – a sight (and smell) to behold. Choose
from rustic Parillas and shabby barbecue grills to
cosy family-run asados and sleek-chic haunts –
the *vacio* (flank steak) is tender whatever the
decor, so ask for it *bien jugoso* (rare) if you dare.

📅 In between the major feasts (when you're hungry), Oct
ℹ️ Uruguay Department of Tourism www.turismo.gub.uy

A meaty haven of succulent steaks and prime ribs

28 Spot Rare Black-necked Cranes | ASIA

Central Bhutan

Considered a Buddhist symbol of peace, Bhutan's
elegant black-necked cranes are one of the world's
most highly endangered bird species. In winter the
scenic alpine valley of Phobjikha in Central Bhutan
is one of the few remaining places where these
graceful birds can settle with ease. Of the 5,000
birds left, over 300 or so overwinter in the Phobjikha
valley where local villagers leave them in gentle
peace. Arrive at the end of October when cranes
can be found throughout marshes and fallow fields.

📅 End of Oct (when the cranes arrive)
ℹ️ Bhutan Tourism www.tourism.gov.bt

The rare and graceful Buddhist symbol of peace

29 Tiger Temple | ASIA

Kanchanaburi Province, Thailand

In the heart of Western Thailand's Kanchanaburi province there is a temple with a difference. For not only is it home to monks, prayer and meditation – but also a population of tigers. For a decade, Tiger Temple has rescued tigers endangered by poaching in the Thai-Burmese jungle region. Today, around 20 fully grown tigers and tiger cubs live within the temple grounds – and are reputed to be tame.

Certainly, visitors can get up close and personal with just a rope to keep them at arm's length. As nocturnal creatures, the tigers tend to laze around in the day, but nonetheless an awe-inspiring encounter.

- Year-round, but Oct is quieter
- Tiger Temple Tours www.tigertemplethailand.com
  Thailand Tourism www.tourismthailand.org

30 Pushkar Camel Fair | ASIA

Rajasthan, India

During the annual Camel Fair, the sleepy town of Pushkar becomes congested with camel traders, sightseers, holy men and street vendors. Once a simple gathering, the Camel Fair has grown into a major event with camel racing, dancing and celebrations in an atmosphere of high excitement. Decorated camels in ribbon-strewn saddles and braided headdresses are bought and sold through rowdy bartering. Tourists can enjoy camel rides or camel treks across the dunes – but many choose simply to absorb Pushkar's chaotic streets.

- 4 days, late Oct to early Nov
- India Tourism www.incredibleindia.org

Camels are decorated with vivid ribbons and saddles for Puskar Fair

31 The Paris Catacombs | EUROPE

France

Bones from over six million bodies adorn the walls of the spook-tacular Catacombs of Paris, where 300 km (186 miles) of dark claustrophobia-inducing passageways echo with the sound of dripping

water – a macabre yet intriguing spectacle that inspired Gaston Leroux to pen *Phantom Of The Opera* after paying a visit. During World War II, the French Resistance used this gloomy disorientating maze as a base for covert operations although the ossuary was originally created as a healthy solution to burying Paris's disease-ridden dead. Hewn from limestone rock, the crypts became a depository for millions of unknown human carcasses in 1786, just as the Revolution gained momentum. Today, equality reigns in this heartless storage system with noble and corrupt, young and old, rich and poor all indistinguishable in death. Only a portion of the catacombs is officially open to the public, but the so-called visitor-friendly section (known as the Denfert-Rochereau Ossuary, or simply the Catacombs) is sufficiently spine-chilling. An easily missed black door in a nondescript building leads to a long spiral staircase. Declaring, "Arrête! C'est ici l'empire de la mort." ("Stop! This is the empire of death."), the entry sign is a dramatic welcor stacks of bones piled up to over 1.5 m (5 ft) The subterranean landscape of Paris is also ho to 2,100 km (1,304 miles) of sewerage tunnels a a metro system of 199 km (125 miles). All three converge at various points and to navigate these eerie labyrnths has become an illicit sport amongst a Parisian subculture, the cataphiles. Anyone prone to hyperventilation or of a nervous disposition should give these tight winding tunnels a miss. On Halloween the setting is at its grisly best.

23 Halloween (open all year)

❶ Guided Tours of the Paris Catacombs

    www.guidedtourparis.com/catacombs.html

    Paris Catacombs www.catacombes-de-paris.fr

A spooky destination for Halloween: the bone-embedded Catacombs

November

1 Day of the Dead

NORTH AMERICA

Oaxaca, Mexico

As November approaches, the smell of incense begins to fill the air in the town of Oaxaca, as people prepare for the Day of the Dead. Stemming from a very human need for transcendence after death, this is one of rural Mexico's most important religious festivals. On the evening of the 31st October, families buy flowers (often marigolds), incense, candles and food and prepare an altar (usually made from a table top). On the morning of November 1st, at the graveside of their loved ones, life is rejoiced – with music, dance and song.

📅 2 days (1st and 2nd Nov)

ℹ️ Mexico Tourism www.visitmexico.com

Deceased friends and relatives are remembered and celebrated

2 Kite Festival

SOUTH AMERICA

Santiago Sacatepéquez, Guatemala

The flying of kites is a popular symbol of communication with the deceased. This is especially true of the Day of the Dead Kite Festival in Santiago Sacatepéquez, when kites are everywhere: big and small, ragged and plain, multicolored and fanciful. People spend the day praying, visiting and eating picnics in the cemetery in remembrance of family members. Then, as the seasonal gusts gather oomph, giant kites fill the air, carrying notes to the dead and to God together with handmade kites of ripped plastic bags, paper and cloth – and whatever else is lying around.

📅 Nov 2nd

ℹ️ Guatemala Tourism www.visitguatemala.com

Kites are flown to symbolize a link between heaven and Earth

3 Leaping Salmon | NORTH AMERICA

Maine, USA

Atlantic salmon is one of Maine's gritty wildlife species – making a two-year-long journey to Greenland and back to spawn in its native river. In the 1940s, landing a 14–18 kg (30–40 lb) salmon here didn't require a knack with a rod and reel and wily patience – just the ability to catch, as runs of 100,000 leaping salmon turned the river into a writhing mass.

Today, numbers are half that amount, but impressive nonetheless. As the fish return, thousands of anglers descend on Grand Lake Stream September-October in order to battle with leaping salmon in fast waters.

📅 Sep – Oct (when salmon are swimming to spawn)

ℹ️ Maine Tourism www.visitmaine.com

4 Ice-breaking and Swimming | EUROPE

Kemi, Finland

At just 30° north of the Arctic Circle, Kemi is surrounded by vast snow fields and frequented by sledge-drivers, husky trains and snowmobiles – a true expedition hub. Kemi is also the launch point for the Sampo Icebreaker – a four-engine vessel triple the size of a standard cargo ship that transports tourists in a series of ear-splitting cracks out on the northern Gulf of Bothnia's vast swathe of ice-capped sea. Passengers don spaceage thermal snowsuits, goggles and helmets to board the 3,450-ton ship in temperatures that hover around 0°C (32°F). It takes four hours to inch through 20 km (12 miles) of thick ice November to the end of April. Swimming in the gulf's bitterly cold waters provides the ultimate Sampo thrill in a skin-tight orange thermal wetsuit. Slide into the sea to float alongside giant chunks of over-sized sorbet - so exciting that you barely feel the cold.

Inch through huge expanses of thick ice in a 3.4 ton icebreaker

📅 Nov – Apr (whenever you travel you'll need to prepare for temperatures from -20°C – -40°C (-4°F– -40°F)

ℹ️ Sampo Tours www.sampotours.com

Finnish Tourist Board www.visitfinland.com

5 Guy Fawkes Night

London, England

Every community in Great Britain celebrates Guy
Fawkes Night (or Bonfire Night) in some form or
other, be it firework displays, huge bonfires or
handheld sparklers at home. Held on the evening
of November 5th, the event marks the foiling of
the Gunpowder Plot on the same date in 1605 in
which Guy Fawkes and his Catholic co-conspirators
attempted to blow-up London's Houses of
Parliament. Rejoicing at the deliverance of the
King was compulsory until 1859.

📅 Nov 5th

ℹ London Tourist Board www.visitlondon.com

Skies burst with fireworks in honour of Guy Fawkes

6 Bungee-jump the Zambezi River

Zimbabwe – Zambia

Bungee nuts ask "why live on the edge, when it's
more fun to leap off" – especially in the awesome
setting of the Victoria Falls. The 111 m (354 ft)
death-defying leap allows several seconds of jaw-
dropping scenery on the plummet towards the
ground – especially in clear, autumn mornings. A
bridge between the Zimbabwean and Zambian
border posts provides the venue. Every jump is
videoed for postrity – encouraging even the jelly-
legged to raise a smile as they plunge.

📅 Nov brings near-hysteria as daily showers arrive – and the locals
rejoice after 2 months of searing, dry heat.

ℹ AFRIZIM (bungee jump tours) www.afrizim.com
SAFPAR (bungee jump tours) www.safpar.com
Zambia Tourism www.zambiatourism.com

Bungee-jumpers have the Victoria Falls as a backdrop

Bahrain International Music Festival | ASIA

Bahrain

Each year since 1990, an invited orchestra is guest of honour at the Bahrain International Music Festival, held in the Bahrain Arts Theatre in Manama in November. In addition to musical contributions from Bahrainian orchestras the festival incorporates an impressive field of international musicians in a broad-based classical programme ranging from chamber music to choral groups together with fresh new talent in a popular youth segment.

📅 Nov

ℹ Bahrain Tourism www.bahraintourism.com

 Swim in Thermal Waters | AUSTRALIA/PACIFIC

Deception Island, Antarctica

Named for navy man Henry Foster's magnetic experiments using pendulums in 1829, Port Foster in Deception Island sits on a gently sloping ash and cinder beach. Dominated by Pendulum Cove, the shallow shoreline is dotted with steaming geothermal pools where temperatures reach around 70°C (158°F). When access allows (Nov – Feb), visitors can take a dip in warm water amongst seismic monitoring stations, rare Antarctic mosses and curious seals in freezing snow.

📅 Nov – Feb

ℹ Deception Island www.deceptionisland.aq

 Bottlenose Dolphins | AUSTRALIA/PACIFIC

Monkey Mia, Western Australia

Monkey Mia, about 850 km (528 miles) north of Perth, is famed for the 300 bottlenose dolphins that frequent its shoreline. In 1964, a local befriended the dolphins. Today, generations have enjoyed regular human contact – an interaction that is now a part of the dolphins' everyday lives. Part of the Shark Bay World Heritage Area, Monkey Mia – and its extraordinary population of cetaceans – is protected, with breeding carefully monitored.

November heralds the arrival of the largest number of newborn – with nursing dolphins and infants often spotted.

📅 Nov (breeding season)

ℹ Shark Bay Research Foundation Monkey Mia
www.monkeymiadolphins.org
Western Australia Tourism www.discoverwest.com.au

10 Day of the Gaucho

San Antonio de Areco, Argentina

Argentina's "Día de la Tradición" (Day of the Tradition) commemorates the 1834 birth of homespun poet José Hernandez, who wrote about gaucho culture in his award-winning book *Martin Fierro*. Today, the cowboys of the pampas get to celebrate their traditions, art, dances and folklore in cattle-roping settlements across Argentina. In San Antonio de Areco, a place where horses outnumber cars, the gaucho party in true cowboy style drinking, dancing and indulging in flamboyant displays of horsemanship. In fact, the Day of the Tradition is a slap-up orgy of all things Argentine from heavy red wine to vast amounts of flame-roasted beef. (Argentines consume an average of 60 kg (132 lb) per year.) While the principal Día de la Tradición is November 10th, the festivities can often stretch over two weekends, climaxing on the final Sunday. Wooden tables are set up round a floodlit plaza for an afternoon feast, preceded by a huge public parade through San Antonio's paved main square – gauchos, horses, women, children, chickens and all.

Nov 10th

Argentina Tourism www.turismo.gov.ar

11 Mani Rimdu at Tengboche Gompa

Nepal

Each year, according to the Tibetan lunar calendar, Sherpas from the Khumbu region congregate for nine days of ceremonies and meditation that mark the Mani Rimdu festival. Tengboche is situated on a spur at 3,870 m (12,697 ft) with views of Mt Everest and Ama Dablam. Ten days of non-stop meditative prayer serve as a prelude to the festivities of Mani Rimdu – chanting monks in flowing robes dancing together with the sound of cymbals, conch shells, horns and flutes.

9 days the full moon of Oct - Nov

Tengboche Monastary www.tengboche.org

Ten days of meditative prayer serve as a prelude to the festivities

12 Karfiguela Waterfalls | AFRICA

Burkino Faso

In the final days of the rainy season, Burkino Faso's Karfiguela Waterfalls lose the unpredictable danger of swollen waters. Torrents begin to steady to a cascade as whitewater spray splashes over massive boulders. During the rains, the dirt tracks that lead to the falls are impassable but by mid-November the mango-tree trail leads straight to a chaotic jumble of rocks. Strip off here, then scramble down to the edge for awesome views.

Nov (immediately after the rains)

Bukino Faso Tourism www.burkina.com

13 Pink Flamingo Spotting | AFRICA

Parc National des Oiseaux du Djoudj, Senegal

Senegal's Djoudj Wetlands sit within the 16,000-hectare (39,500 acre) Djoudj National Bird Sanctuary where boggy inland deltas lie in the flood-plain of the Senegal River. The third most important reserve of its kind in the world, the sanctuary is on the border with Mauritania, around a huge lake. As the first wetland area south of the Sahara, the sanctuary attracts around three-million migratory species from Europe. Over 1.5 million birds call the sanctuary home including the white pelican, purple heron, African spoonbill and cormorant. But of the 400 species found here, the pink flamingos are a highlight. Find them in huge numbers in November, provided the autumn in Europe hasn't been too mild.

Nov (Flamingo season)

Senegal Tourism www.senegal-tourism.com

14 The Northern Lights | EUROPE

Svalbard, Norway

Only the very hardy visit Svalbard (meaning cold edge) during wintertime. Yet this archipelago between the northern tip of Norway and the North Pole boasts a certain charm in the depths of winter – even though the sun never gets off the ground. Arrive in a swaddle of thermal clothes to survive average temperatures of -20°C (-4°F) and keep your wits about you as the town is on constant high-alert for polar bear incursions. A more welcomed visitor is the green, red, blue, violet and yellow sparkle of the Northern Lights (the aurora borealis), a dazzling VIP guest to this snow-covered expanse enveloped by darkness – and in Svalbard, darkness means darkness: no twilight, no dusk, just the glow of the moon and the smallest twinkle of the stars.

Winter (it's tourist-free but only for hardy souls)

Svalbard Tourism www.svalbard.net

15 Flowers in the Desert

Kalahari Game Reserve, Botswana

Dusty plains, saltpans, sand dunes, scrubland and long dried-out riverbeds characterise the Kalahari Game Reserve. The climate can be harsh with temperatures in the shade exceeding 40°C (104°F) during the summer (November to April), while ground temperatures hit a whopping 70°C (158°F). Rainfall is erratic, but mainly arrives between November and April, after which grass and flowers transform the landscape – before drying out again. But for this brief period, Kalahari Game Reserve yields to its alter ego – a lush meadow-country of plump shoots and blooms. Large herds of gemsboks and springboks come to graze, while lions, cheetahs and jackals follow the herbivores. Giraffe, warthog, brown hyaena, African wild dog, leopard, wildebeest, eland, kudu and red hartebeest can also be seen.

23 Month-long, mid Nov to mid-Dec only

🛈 Botswana Tourism www.botswanatourism.co.bw

Green shoots, grass and flowers transform the desert in the wets

16 Tea-tasting

Galle, Sri Lanka

In ancient China, tea was revered for its medicinal powers while in Boston, USA it destroyed a symbol of 18th century colonial rule. Wars have been fought over it; traders have battled buccaneer-infested seas for it. Entire communities are built around its rituals. Today, tea is the glue that binds Sri Lankan society together. In searing heat under an egg-yolk sun, lips cracked, throat parched and with saliva in short supply, tea is a welcomed thirst-quenching libation – as Sri Lanka's 19-million tea drinkers will testify. Since the days of British rule, Sri Lanka's 160-year-old tea industry has become a major player with its finest teas produced from bushes that grow above 1,219 m (4,000 ft). In the cool, tea grows slowly and is tricky to harvest due to the steep angle of the slopes. Six main tea-producing areas include historic Galle, to the south. Here, at the Tittagalla Tea Estate, Tamil tea pluckers scour the hill-country bushes filling baskets with two-leaves-and-a-bud on one of the few tea plantations close to the sea. It also produces the world's most expensive White tea at $US 1500 a kilo. Sri Lankan plantations employ a total workforce of well over a million people each estate distinctive for its own individual flavour, aroma, and colour.

Tea Estate owner's have come up with an answer to wine tourism offered by European countries, opening up tea houses and tasting rooms to honour Sri Lanka's most popular beverage. Pale-gold brews are poured from large brass kettles via gleaming fine-holed strainers. Floral aromas mix with subtle flinty tangs as delicate flavours swirl around the mouth. Tea is weighed out with precision before being steeped in near-boiling water for five minutes, then poured. Guided by tea masters, novices are encouraged to heighten their smell, sight, touch and taste. After being strained out into white ceramic bowls, experts will slurp and grade, inspecting the infusions for colour and nose, much like a fine Bordeaux. Slosh it around in the mouth to oxidize the liquid and release its intensity – then it's time to savour the fullest flavours from the brew.

📅 Nov – Dec

ℹ️ Sri Lanka Tourism www.srilankatourism.org

17 Toronto Sketch Comedy Festival | NORTH AMERICA

Canada

Dozens of workshops shift the focus away from the six days of first-rate comedy on stage at Toronto's Comedy Sketch Festival with mentoring for would-be comics a major draw. Group sessions allow audiences and comedians alike to examine the 'nuts and bolts' of sketch comedy – while seminars look at producing comedy, creating a buzz, relationships with media, editing scripts and a director's role. Oh, then there are the parties – a mix of networking, beer-swilling and swotting up on fresh material.

📅 6 days, mid Nov

ℹ️ Toronto Sketch Comedy Festival
www.torontosketchfest.com

18 Pirate Week | NORTH AMERICA

Cayman Islands

Despite the Cayman Island's reputation for tax-free wheeler-dealing, this ten-day festival isn't to honour the cut-throat piracy of its offshore bankers, but a celebration of the swashbuckling seamen that once plundered the shores. The Cayman Islands kick off events with a mock pirate invasion staged by old-time sailing vessels, loaded with gun-toting mariners. Expect live Caribbean music, street dancing, costumed parades and fireworks together with a popular cardboard boat race – on a pirate theme, of course.

📅 11 days mid-Nov

ℹ️ Pirates Week Festival www.piratesweekfestival.com
Cayman Island Tourism www.caymanislands.ky

19 Kapono Ukulele Festival | AUSTRALIA/PACIFIC

New Zealand

Expect some show-stopping headline acts at New Zealand's celebration of the ukulele each November, when youngsters and maestros alike pay tribute to the instrument's global resurgence. At the forefront of the revival are Pacific Island musicians, lending the Hawaiian word Kapono to the event (meaning a little piece of heaven). The ukulele may be a humble four-stringed instrument, but performances are big on sound and splendour featuring both world renowned Uke players and hundreds of school-age musicians.

📅 Nov (varies)

ℹ️ Kiwi Ukulele www.kiwiukulele.com

New Zealand Tourism www.newzealand.com

20 Water Festival | ASIA

Phnom Penh, Cambodia

Few other gatherings in the Khmer calendar are as exuberant as Cambodia's Bon Om Tuk (Water Festival), a 400-boat regatta on the banks of Phnom Penh's Tonle Sap River. Held late October or November, up to a million spectators watch Cambodia's boatmen battle for top honours. People pour into the capital to cheer on their local team – leaving villages empty as the city's population almost doubles. Elaborate dug-out canoes have brightly-painted eyes on the prows to ward off evil spirits. Boats are raced in pairs along a kilometre-long (half mile) course as oarsmen frantically paddle and chant in fierce competition. An evening pageant of decorated floats is illuminated by fireworks, heralding the nightly drinking, music, feasting and dancing. Dating back to the era of King Jayavarman II, the 9th century founder of the great Angkorian Empire, the festival marks the changing flow of the Tonle Sap River. This remarkable phenomenon sees the course reverse as the rainy season progresses. Fortuitously, the Water Festival also coincides with the full moon of the Buddhist month of Kadeuk – a good omen that promises a bountiful harvest.

📅 Full moon, late Oct or early Nov

ℹ️ Cambodia Tourism www.tourismcambodia.com

Hand-hollowed wooden boats highly decorated to ward off evil

21 Beaujolais Run

London, England – Reims, France

Each year, the onset of British winter brings thoughts of a wacky 1,000-car race – all in the name of French wine. An oddball assortment of competitors from all walks of life begin planning their cross-channel strategies in secret rendezvous as they fine-tune plans for the madcap Beaujolais Run. First staged in 1972 when *Sunday Times* journalist Alan Hall threw down the gauntlet to Fleet Street to deliver the first bottle of Beaujolais to his desk, speed was once of the essence. The challenge was taken up by the RAF who broke all the records in a Harrier jet – a loophole that's been closed.

Today, the starter's flag comes down as all manner of vehicles, from rusty wrecks to Lamborghinis, make a bid for the Channel tunnel. In this all-for-fun-and-charity rally, each entrant needs to raise $US 750 (£500) with the expectation that they'll at least double that in sponsorship for charities Great Ormond Street Hospital and the Down's Syndrome Association. Fancy dress is de rigueur so a motley crew of tutu-wearing fairies, nuns, 007s and Disney characters descend on the A26 motorway. Drivers follow a series of cryptic clues around obscure back-roads and random locations to reach Reims and claim the Beaujolais at midnight, in time for the return leg a 550 km (341 mile) sprint in which navigational agility wins out.

📅 3rd Tuesday in Nov (3 – 4 days)

ℹ️ Beaujolais Run www.beaujolaisrun.com
Beaujolais Tourism www.beaujolais.com

22 Beaujolais Nouveau Day

Beaujeu, France

For over 55 years, the arrival of the season's Beaujolais Nouveau has been heralded with revelry every third Thursday in November in France – and the world. For centuries, farmhands gulped down this light, fruity just-off-the-vine libation to celebrate the end of the harvest. Today, the latest vintage is embraced across the world as speedier delivery services allow other nations to join in. Produced from the Gamay grape in a hilly area just north of Lyon, Beaujolais Nouveau is not a complex tipple – but more the everyday drink of masses. French law dictates that the new Beaujolais cannot be served before that magic Thursday – so the countdown for a midnight sip begins on Wednesday evening. In the home of Beaujolais in south-eastern France the young wine's arrival signifies the biggest celebration in the calendar with local restaurants packed to capacity. Beaujeu, the region's capital, hosts a big party or Sarmentelles, so named from the French word for the grapevine canes (sarments) that are set alight in the centre of town. Amidst huge crowds, Beaujeu's barrels are opened to loud cheers as the party begins and the new vintage is fully indulged.

📅 3rd Thursday in Nov

ℹ️ Beaujolais Tourism www.beaujolais.com

23 Sunset at the Salar de Uyuni | SOUTH AMERICA

Uyuni, Bolivia

Words defy even the most powerful literary pen when it comes to describing Bolivia's Salar de Uyuni, the largest salt lake on earth at around 12,000 sq km (7456 miles). Set at 3,600 m (11,811 ft) above sea level, this vast expanse is the result of the slow evaporation of Largo Tayca – a giant salt-water basin that vanished, leaving a barren, mineral rich moonscape terrain in its wake. Extraordinary geological features give Salar de Uyuni an eerie, unearthly appearance with spouting geysers, spurting hot springs and fumaroles on a shimmering landscape tinged with crimson pink. Located in the southwest of Bolivia, near the crest of the Andes, the composition of the flats is mind-boggling with high concentrations of halite and gypsum in a salt-crusted, sun-bleached skeletal desert that has been cured by thin dry air.

At sunset the largest salt lake on Earth boasts an ethereal glow accross crystal-crusted crags and wind-blown subterranean fissures

Swept by high winds, the Salar de Uyuni is Martian in its appearance, save a few cactus-hemmed pools, with plum-purple, gust-blown crags that leave explorers gasping for breath. Boasting an extraordinary clarity, the deep blue of the altiplano sky is often completely without cloud. Rocky plateaus form a fringe around views that are nothing less than staggering. Gurgling mud pools hide amongst fiery-red canyons close to algae-rich waters trickling through subterranean fissures. At sunrise, gentle whisps of smoke puff into the pastel glow as flamingos study their reflections in the moisture – an almost hallucinogenic vision in this serene world.

🗓 July – Nov (winter) when the surface is dry

❶ Bolivia Tourism www.turismobolivia.bo

Bolivia Expeditions www.bolivianexpeditions.com

Uyuni Natours www.uyuni.com.bo

24 Christmas Markets

Vienna, Austria

At the onset of Advent, Vienna's "Christkindlmärkte" (Christmas Markets) begin spreading across the city's snow-chilled streets amidst steaming spiced wine stalls and "Würstelstand" (sausage vendors). A centuries-old tradition since Emperor Albrecht I granted a 'Dezembermarkt' (December market) in 1296, the markets attract festive shoppers in their droves. Choose from a wide range of handicrafts, candied fruit, pastries and roasted chestnuts. Fairy lights and Christmas trees decorate every square with traditional carols sung by Sunday choirs at venues city-wide.

🗓 Late Nov – Dec 24th

ℹ Vienna Tourism www.wien.info
   Austria National Tourist Office www.austria.info

Vienna's streetscape is enlived by fairy-lights, candles and roasting chestnuts

25 Dean's Blue Hole

The Bahamas

Close to the shallow waters near the bay west of Long Island's Clarence Town, the alabaster sandy sea bottom suddenly drops away to disappear into a dark, blue void. At 202 m (663 ft), Dean's Blue Hole is a chasm so dramatic it creates tidal surges powerful enough to capsize a boat. Yet, chose a time wisely (November is calm and clear) and it is possible to navigate the strong currents as a diver – twice a day. Today, the site is popular with free-divers who use breath-holding techniques to enter this extraordinary universe of stalactites, darting fish and other marine life.

📅 Year-round (waters in Nov – Jan are calm and clear)

ℹ️ Bahamas Tourism www.bahamas.com

26 Secret Postcard Sale

Royal College of Art, England

One of the UK's most distinctive annual art events, London's Royal College of Art's Secret Sale is ingeniously simple. Around 2,500 postcards – some created by established artists, other by students – go on sale in November. Each is sold for £40 ($US 65) and signed on the reverse. To date, sales of postcards have topped £1 million ($US 1.5 million), helping hundreds of emerging artists. The identity of the artists is revealed only once the artwork is bought.

📅 1 day sale at end of 7 day on-line viewing, mid-Nov

ℹ️ Royal College of Art www.rca.ac.uk

Can you spot a master in the making?

27 Thanksgiving

Cranberry Islands, Maine, USA

The largest of Maine's five Cranberry Islands are Great Cranberry and Little Cranberry. Native Americans lived here long before the first European settlers arrived. Today, the islands and their close-knit community of lobstermen and artists boast an off-the-beaten-track sleepy ambience. A year-round population of around 100 people (and just a handful of roads) makes it a cozy (and aptly named) place to celebrate Thanksgiving amidst wooden over-the-water fishing huts and quaint cottages.

📅 Fourth Thursday in Nov

ℹ️ Cranberry Isles www.cranberryisles-me.gov

28 Death Valley by Motorbike

California, USA

One of America's finest 'winter parks', Death Valley is one of the hottest, driest ecosystems in the country. Superlatives abound when describing this rugged 1.2 million hectare (3 million acre) wonderland with its rolling sand dunes, snow-capped mountains, multi-coloured rock strata and plunging ravines. Over 1 million people explore Death Valley's harsh desert each year, home to the Timbisha Shoshone and unique plants and animals. In the week after Thanksgiving, the salt pans are near-empty – a 64 km (40 mile)-long by 8 km (5 mile)- wide, expanse best explored on a Harley Davidson amidst racing road-runners and coyote.

23 Immediately after Thanksgiving – the quietest time of the year

ⓘ Death Valley National Park www.nps.gov/deva

Roar through the multi-coloured rock strata, plunging ravines and rolling sand dunes

29 King Penguins | SOUTH AMERICA

South Georgia

Renowned as a wildlife paradise where whales gather and millions of seals thrive, South Georgia Island is home to wandering albatross – and four different species of penguins (Macaroni, gentoo, chinstrap and king). The king penguin is the second largest of the living penguin species (the emperor being the largest) at around 15 kg (33 lbs) and just under a metre (3 ft) tall. Characterized by big splashes of orange and yellow feathers around their heads and necks, they are distinguished in appearance (hence the name).

South Georgia Island is located 1,390 km (863 miles) southeast of the Falkland Islands and 2,150 km (1,335 miles) from South America – a remoteness that has helped protect its birds and marine life. Without an airstrip, the only mode of transport is boat, making it a destination for intrepid tourists only. Most arrive on icebreakers or vessels large enough to brave the rough passage to the island – conditions

are bad enough to render even the crustiest old seadog seriously green around the gills. However, the tumultuous swells are well worth suffering for an opportunity to witness 600,000 king penguins on the island's Salisbury Plain with their furry, brown chicks huddling for warmth in the Arctic breeze. On South Georgia Island, most are found near streams flowing from glaciers, allowing the kings to waddle down to the sea in groups for a splash and bob about. Breeding takes place north of the pack ice on islands around the Antarctic convergence with each pair rearing two chicks in around three years in separate hatchings. Breeding times can vary in the colonies and kings can be at different stages of development in a single site: some may be incubating eggs while others are moulting and some mating.

📅 Nov (summer)

ℹ️ South Georgia Island Tourism www.sgisland.org

30 Steamboat up the Mississippi | NORTH AMERICA

New Orleans, USA

Anyone who's read a Mark Twain novel knows what it's like to pine for a journey on the mighty Mississippi in a paddle-wheel steamboat. Indeed his *nom de plume* (his real name was Samuel Clemens) was a term he learned from steamboat passion. 'Mark twain' means two fathoms, or 12 feet of water in the age of paddle-wheel travel. In Twain's evocative novel *The Steamboat Race*, he evokes the nostalgia of wheel-powered river-hauled cargoes of cotton and

sugar. Today, the Mississippi River is still synonymous with steam-propelled travel – the perfect way to sightsee New Orleans' stretch of this scenic 3,770 km (6,067 mile) expanse on Mark Twain's birthday.

📅 Nov 30th (Mark Twain's birthday)

ℹ️ Mississippi Tourism www.visitmississippi.org
   Paddleford River Cruises www.riverrides.com
   Lacrosse Queen River Cruises www.lacrossequeen.com

Luminescent Plankton

SOUTH AMERICA

Punta Vieja, Panama

Choose a calm night with a plump, full moon to take a dip off the shores off Isla Bastimentos at Punta Vieja (Old Point) to swim in inky-black waters illuminated by a stunning constellation of phosphorescent plankton, flickering like organic fairy lights in the dark. In the glowing, warm depths these soft pinprick-sized glows fill the waters as far as the eye can see. Dive down into the depths to become immersed in living sparks of sparkling, neon-like bright green – a glittering mass that can attach itself to the human body in a fuzzy other-worldly glow.

Bioluminescence is a primarily marine phenomenon produced by dinoflagellate algae – microscopic single-celled organisms that form a major part of the phytoplankton at the base of most aquatic food chains. It is the predominant source of light in the largest fraction of the habitable volume of the earth – the deep ocean. Bioluminescence is the production and emission of light by a living organism as the result of a chemical reaction during which chemical energy is converted to light energy by a series of chemical reactions.

In the waters off Punta Vieja, thick swirls radiate in dazzling clouds churned into luminosity by the tides. A clap of the hands creates an underwater galaxy that makes skin glow like stardust, heightened by the shimmers of an egg-yolk moon. Part of the 13,000 hectare (32,123 acre) Bastimentos National Marine Park, Punta Vieja boasts a magical aura enhanced by remote peacefulness, white sandy beaches and wild, tangled mangrove forests rich in wildlife, including turtles, dolphins and many more.

📅 Year-round, though Nov is quiet
ℹ️ Bastimentos National Marine Park
  www.bastimentosnationalmarinepark.com

2 Perang Topat

ASIA

Lombok, Bali, Indonesia

In Pura Lingsar, about 10 km (6 miles) from the town of Mataram, farmers throw Ketupat (steamed rice wrapped in palm leaves) at each other during Perang Topat (Topat War) to bring prosperity to the coming year. Held at the multi-faith Lingsar temple, the celebrations are a demonstration of the harmonious relationship between local Hindus and Muslims.

Rituals take place in the temple's outer courtyard where both faiths prepare their respective offerings of sweet cakes, fruit and two buffaloes.

📅 Three days before Dec full moon
ℹ️ Indonesia Tourism www.my-indonesia.info

3 Waltz Season

Vienna, Austria

At the first early signs of winter, Vienna turns all thoughts to the upcoming Ball Season. Once deemed too risqué to be danced by couples other than those married to each other, the Viennese Waltz's sinful holds earned it persecution for vulgarity. Today couples are free to enjoy Vienna's spirited 180 beats-per-minute-romps without fear of incarceration – a liberty that the Viennese pursue with a passion. Derived from the German "walzen" meaning to roll, turn, or glide, the Viennese Waltz is a fast-tempo rotary dance packed with change steps and turns that requires light, nimble feet – quite unlike the sluggish pace of its more sedate British namesake.

Vienna's dazzling three-month ball season is a joyous social whirl as more than 300 events issue thousands of gilded invitations to ball-goers city-wide. Before the balls get into full swing on 31st December, the Viennese book classes to brush up on their technique with newbie dancers and refresher students alike, seeking the guidance of Thomas Schäfer-Elmayer – a judge on Austrian TV's 'Dancing Stars'. Coaching sessions begin in early December.

📅 Dec (practice month) before ball season starts Dec 31st ('til end of Mar)

ℹ️ Elmayer Dance School www.elmayer.at
Vienna Tourist Board www.wien.info

Ball season in Vienna is a social whirl of dazzling waltzing extravaganzas

4 Giant Statues

AUSTRALIA/PACIFIC

Theories abound on the mystic origins of Easter Island's statues

Easter Island

Located 3,500 km (2,174 miles) off the coast of Chile, Easter Island is the world's most remote inhabited island – technically a conjoined trio of extinct volcanoes that rise over 3,500 m (10,000 ft) from the ocean floor. Fodder for widespread speculation, the cultural development of Easter Island is shrouded myth in relation to its giant statues dating back to AD700 – some of which are over 1.2 m (4 ft) tall and weigh around 14 tons. Theories as to how the rock-hewn figures were carved then hauled and erected range from ship-wrecked elephants to Atlantis and arrivals from another world. Conjecture continues regarding mystic energy fields, alien influence and spiritual dynamics – one of the planet's last great puzzles.

📅 Avoid the festival of Tapati (between late Jan and early Feb) when crowds swell, Dec is nicer and much, much quieter.
ℹ Chile Tourism www.visit-chile.org

5 Chasing the Claus

EUROPE

Switzerland

Traditional Klausjagen celebrations begin at sunset when an illuminated procession takes to the streets. Originally an ancient pagan custom to banish winter spirits, Klausjagen now incorporates Christian themes. Santa Claus cuts a dignified figure, followed by a calvalcade of musicians and torch-bearers. Then, a group of "Santa Chasers" – sometimes as many as several hundred men – who ring their bells in rhythmic unison before a mass blowing of horns.

📅 Dec 5th
ℹ Klausjagen (Chasing the Claus) www.klausjagen.ch

Ancient pagan rituals and Christian teachings combine

6 Jellyfish Lake

Palau

Jellyfish Lake is one of around 70 marine lakes scattered throughout a limestone archipelago in the Pacific pockmarked with sinkholes and porous with caves and tunnels cut by flowing fresh water during past ice ages, Ongeim'l Tketau can only be accessed by traversing a ridge that separates the lake from the surrounding lagoon. Rope guides highlight the path and provide added stability on a rocky jungle terrain rich in lizards, snakes and birds. Climb onto a mossy wooden dock to look out onto waters filled with 10-million golden jellyfish that follow the path of the sun as it crosses the lake.

Sunlight is an essential element in the lives of the golden jellyfish, which derive their colour and much of their energy from intracellular algae. As the sun rises, the jellyfish begin their migration in the western basin, where they overnight to reach the furthest illuminated edges of the eastern basin by mid-morning. They then reverse their course to return to the western basin by mid-afternoon to complete 1 km (0.6 mile) trip that keeps them in the sun and away from the predatory anemone in the dark edges of the lake. Thousands of visitors arrive Ongeim'l Tketau to swim among the jellyfish, sponges, sea squirts, mussels, anemones, and algae spectacularly illuminated by the beams of sunlight. Contrary to popular belief, the jellyfish aren't "stingless" but their stinging cells (nematocysts) are so tiny that the sting is almost impossible to detect. Avoid touching the jellyfish, as this can damage them.

23 Palau's heaviest rainfalls have been and gone by the end of Dec (start May)

ⓘ Pala Tourist Office www.visit-palau.com

Swim among jellyfish illuminated by spectacular shafts of light

7 **Wrangler National Finals Rodeo** | NORTH AMERICA

Las Vegas, USA

The ten-day NFR has been thrilling Las Vegas during early December since 1959 – and more than 50 years on this edge-of-your-seat spectacle remains a major draw. The Thomas & Mack Centre becomes 'Cowboy Central' complete with lassoes, leather chaps, whips and 10-gallon Stetsons as gold buckle dreams are realized by a skilled elite. Some 120 cowboys and cowgirls from all over the world sling it out in a showdown of steer wrestling, roping, bareback riding, bull-riding and saddle bronc riding – and with US$5 million of prize money up for grabs it's a hotly contested challenge.

📅 4th – 13th Dec (9 days)

ℹ️ Pro Rodeo www.prorodeo.com
    Las Vegas Tourism www.visitlasvegas.com

Saddle up for seat-of-your-pants excitement at the main event

8 **Luna Runtun Spa** | SOUTH AMERICA

Ecuador

Ecuador's mountainous Baños region is rich in indigenous history from the ancient rope-weaving Puruhá people to the Huambaloes who travelled with the Spanish conquistadors. High on the Andean peaks, set amongst thickets and craggy boulders, the region's tambos (wooden lodges) offered a resting spot for travellers traversing the pre-Incan mountain trails between the Amazon Basin and the Andes. Today, the region is part of the 271,000-hectare (700,000 acre) Sangay National Park and home of the Luna Runtun Adventure Spa where

medicinal plants, fruits, volcanic stones, molten ashes, clay, mud and vegetables from a 25.5 hectare (63 acre) organic garden are used in natural healing therapies. Guests can enjoy sunrise breathing exercises in pure morning air before restorative treatments using crystal-clear mineral waters from the Tungurahua springs.

📅 During short dry season, Dec – Jan

ℹ️ Luma Runtun Adventure Spa www.lunaruntun.com

9 Christmas Walkabout | NORTH AMERICA

Bermuda

Hosted by the Bermuda National Trust, the annual Christmas Walkabout in St George's explores some of the festively-lit buildings and plazas, from the yuletide bands in Water Street and Kings Square and the school choirs of the Unfinished Church to the arts, crafts and Christmas baked goods at St Peter's Church Hall.

🗓 1 day, early Dec

ℹ Bermuda Tourism www.bermudatourism.com

10 Whirling Dervishes Festival | EUROPE

Konya, Turkey

Over a million people descend on Konya, the ancient Seljuk capital, for the festival of the Whirling Dervishes – an incredible 700-year-old spectacle held to commemorate the Sufic saint Mevlana, popularly known as Rumi (AD1207-1273). The great academic and philosopher Mevlana (meaning "Our Lord" in Arabic) believed a spiritual connectivity could be achieved with God through dance. Known as "Sema", the dance is believed by the Sufis to have originated when the universe came into being. The climax of the festival, the 'Nuptial Night', commemorates the death of Mevlana and his union with God. Dancers wear highly symbolic clothing: cloaks represent a coffin, conical shaped hats a gravestone and white skirts a shroud. The leader symbolizes the sun and the dancers spinning around him, the orbits of the moon and stars. To begin each phase of the dance, the dervishes kiss the right hand of the Sheikh (the Mevlevi sect's religious leader) before bowing, then beginning to whirl. Right palms face towards heaven to receive God's goodness while left palms face the earth in order to distribute it. Four different dances symbolize the four seasons, the four elements and the four ages of man. Their long white skirts spinning like splayed fans, the dancers whirl and move anti-clockwise while maintaining their position with respect to the others, matching the revolution of the universe.

The 700 year-old festival attracts more than 1 million visitors

🗓 8 days, 9th – 17th Dec

ℹ Turkey Tourism www.tourismturkey.org

11 Tea at the Peninsular Hotel | ASIA

Hong Kong

Taking High Tea in grand 1920s style in Hong Kong's Peninsula Hotel is as grand a tradition as they come. Expect antique furniture, brass, marble and oodles of opulence under neo-classical arches, as three-tiered British high tea sets are filled and Earl Grey tea poured. Nibble on bite-sized sandwiches, pink frosted cakes and cream-topped jam-filled scones.

Pleasantries are exchanged to the gentle accompaniment of a string quartet – and the occasional pop of a Champagne cork.

📅 Nov – Dec (when there's a pleasant breeze through the city)
🛈 Hong Kong Tourism www.discoverhongkong.com
   Peninsula Hotel www.peninsula.com

12 Cruise the Nile | AFRICA

Luxor, Egypt

Traversing about 1,600 km (746 miles) northward from the Egyptian-Sudanese border to the Mediterranean Sea, the Nile River flows across the Sahara to Egypt bringing life to this dry desert region. Lush, green palms bear testament to the fertility and productivity of the land in the Nile River Valley where temperatures can reach over 40°C (113°F). Over 300 riverboats cruise the Nile each

year to visit the temples and tombs of Luxor, built on the site of the ancient city of Thebes. Visit in December when temperatures are a pleasing 25°C (77°F).

📅 Dec, when temperatures are pleasant
🛈 Luxor Tourist Office www.luxorguide.com

13 Tsukiji Fish Market | ASIA

Tokyo, Japan

Much of the silvery, oily fish, plump, translucent roes and succulent shellfish in Tokyo's Tsukiji Fish Market hail from the ultra-fertile waters of Hakkaido, second largest of Japan's four main islands. Not only is Hokkaido a major source of supply to the biggest wholesale fish and seafood market in the world – but it is also the mainstay of Japan's many seafood dishes. In December, the market awaits the arrival of squid (eaten grilled, boiled or pickled, but best of all as sashimi), surf

clams and scallops – all adored winter specialities. Though eaten as sashimi and sushi, squid are often steamed with sake and soya sauce as a rare treat and served and eaten mainly in December – when stocks are fresh.

📅 Dec (when squid's in season)
🛈 Tsukiji Fish Market www.tsukiji-market.or.jp
   Japan National Tourist Office www.jnto.go.jp

14 Ice Hotel

Jukkasjärvi, Sweden

With its snow-covered landscape of frosted pine trees, frozen rivers and icicles, Lapland is the quintessential winter wonderland where sub-zero temperatures shiver as low as -50°C (-58°F). Under the eerie glow of Sweden's polar skies, the Ice Hotel is a giant magical igloo built each November from ice blocks taken from the frozen Torne River. Hand-crafted ice pillars and ice-hewn furniture are strung together with glowing fibre optic cables. The ethereal northern lights can also been seen in this luminescent location 160 km (100 miles) above the Arctic Circle. Make full use of the skis, sleighs and dog-sleds to explore Lapland's reindeer trails and icy wilds. After several warming drinks from the Absolute Ice Bar spend a night snuggled into a thermal sleeping bag under reindeer-skin rugs. Guests are awarded a certificate after surviving plummeting temperatures and are encouraged to thaw out in a pre-breakfast sauna. The beauty, the cold and the quick morning escape are all part of the fun. Come May, or earlier (should there be an unforeseen heat-wave) the walls begin to melt – and that is it for the Ice Hotel until it is time to rebuild the following year.

📅 Early Dec – end of Apr (sometimes early May)

ℹ Ice Hotel www.icehotel.com

Sweden Tourism www.visitsweden.com

Fairytale laser-lit igloos are hewn from ice blocks at -50°C (-58°F)

15 Panama Canal Transit | SOUTH AMERICA

Panama

December marks the month in 1999 when the Panama Canal was handed over to local control by the US. For many of Panama's 3.1 million inhabitants, the change of ownership marked the moment of true independence: a reunification of their homeland and reclamation of the most famous short-cut in the world. Today, millions of visitors enjoy a morning transit on Panama's 'Big Ditch' journeying through a trio of locks banked by jungle and towering tropical palms. At each lock passengers clamour for photographs to the sound of honking horns and clanging bells. It takes a full day (and 127 million litres (52 million gallons) of water) for each vessel to transit the canal. A staggering 900-plus species of migratory and indigenous bird species have been recorded in Panama in single day – many of them in the foliage-rich canal basin in December. Transit passengers should have a pair of binoculars at the ready as the boat edges past Contractor Hill – a haven for cormorants.

📅 Saturdays year round, except May (but Dec – Mar best for wildlife, weather and full transits)

ℹ️ Panama Canal Authority www.pancanal.com
Panama Marine Tours www.pmatours.net
Canal Museum www.canalmuseum.com

16 Volleyball and Cachaca | SOUTH AMERICA

Ipanema Beach, Rio de Janeiro, Brazil

Described as the 'Sexiest Beach in the World', Rio's Ipanema is famous for its dental-floss bikinis, skimpy G-strings, bronzed toned bodies and samba beats. Immortalised by Vinícius de Morais and Antonio Carlos Jobim's 1960s hit "The Girl from Ipanema", this lively spot boasts beautiful weather, beautiful powder-fine white sand and truly beautiful people. On a stunning backdrop of mountains, tropical flora and sweeping ocean views, vendors keep the beach bodies supplied with potent cachaca (sugarcane rum, sugar and lime), splicing coconuts with machetes to the cheers of a well-heeled volleyball crowd.

📅 Dec – Mar

ℹ️ Insiders Guide to Ipanema www.ipanema.com
Department of Tourism www.brazil.org.uk

17 Pilgrimage of St Lazarus | SOUTH AMERICA

El Rincon, Cuba

Thousands of Cuban pilgrims travel on foot to the shrine of St Lazarus (San Lazario), while others, dressed in sackcloth, crawl for miles on bleeding hands and knees. Each pays tribute to St Lazarus, fulfilling vows and seeking favours from the crippled icon immortalized in a giant statue in the dusty farming village of El Rincon.

📅 Dec 17th

ℹ️ Cuba Tourist Office www.cubatravel.cu

18 Mangrove Diving

St. John's Hurricane Hole, US Virgin Islands

On the north-eastern side of St John on the US Virgin Isles lies the knotted gnarl of mangroves at Hurricane Hole. During the threat of a hurricane, boats would head to this tangled shelter to hunker down. Today, as a Coral Reef Monument, Hurricane Hole is untroubled by vessels – and a calm, clear-water paradise popular with mangrove divers for its mesmerizing array of fish, invertebrates, sponges, coral and plants.

📅 Dec – Feb (coolest months at 25°C (77°F))
ℹ US Virgin Islands Tourism www.usvitourism.vi

19 Dickensian Festival of Christmas

Portsmouth, England

Portsmouth plays host to a Dickensian Festival of Christmas at the town's Historic Dockyard amidst stalls of Victoriana foods and costumed merry makers. Punch and Judy shows entertain Portsmouth's tiny urchins together with street jugglers and a host of colourful Dickens characters. On this day in 1843, *A Christmas Carol* was first published in Britain and Dickens, who was born in Portsmouth (1812-1870), is honoured in a month-long jamboree that includes a flea circus and a parade to Fagan's tavern.

📅 Dec (all month)
ℹ Portsmouth Festival of Christmas
www.christmasfestival.co.uk
Portsmouth Tourism www.visitportsmouth.co.uk

20 Balinese Cuisine

Bali, Indonesia

In 1990 Swiss-born Heinz von Holzen arrived in Bali to learn its food traditions. Today, the award-winning chef and food author owns the famous Bumbu Bali Restaurant & Cooking School. Using age-old recipes and traditional cooking techniques, he creates authentic Balinese cuisine - and encourages tourists to discover the island's spicy culinary secrets. Morning visits to local markets allow vegetable and fruit growers and fishermen to share their tales before a chance to recreate Bali's specialities under Heinz's expert guidance. Try Lawar Kuwir (duck sate with green papayas), Sop Ayam (chicken soup with vegetables, noodles and egg), Pesan Be Pasih (banana-wrapped grilled fish) and Hasil Laut Bumbu Kuning (seafood in yellow turmeric sauce).

📅 For a great array of fish and produce, visit Apr – Dec
ℹ Heinz Von Holzen (Cooking School) www.indo-chef.com

1 Rocket Launches | SOUTH AMERICA

Centre Spatial, Guyana

When Algeria gained independence in 1962, the European Space Agency (CNES, Centre National d'Etudes Spatiales) needed to establish an alternative base near to the Equator in a zone that could facilitate all missions into space. After weighing up Trinidad, Brazil and Somalia – amongst others – a deal was struck with French Guyana in 1964. Kourou is perfect for launches and the site is now a world-renowned centre of excellence with an impressive four-decade history of propelling payloads into space using Vega, Soyuz and Ariane launchers. Visitors can witness these space-bound launches after a tour of the Jupiter Control Room and gigantic Ariane 5 facilities – though these must be pre-booked. Arrive in clear, dry weather and the CARAPA observation site offers a jaw-dropping view – without time limit, age restriction, permit or cost.

📅 Year-round, but more launches in Dec
ℹ️ Centre Spatial Guyanais (CSG) www.cnes.fr

22 Hike Tiger Leaping Gorge | ASIA

China

Wedged between the Jade Dragon Snow and Haba Mountains in South West China, the Tiger Leaping Gorge, a 16 km (10 mile) fissure running along the upper reaches of the Yangtze River, is the deepest gorge in the world, boasting more than 20 frothing rapids under a perilous 200 m (665 ft) drop. According to legend, a tiger used a large rock on the gorge's narrowest section as a stepping stone to leap from side to side – hence the name. Steep, roughly hewn trails hug the rushing waters as they slam into rocks and crash into whirlpools. Best in dry, clear weather from October to January.

📅 Oct – Jan (bloom filled and scenic)
ℹ️ China National Tourist Office www.cnto.org
Tiger Leaping Gorge Guiding Service
www.tigerleapinggorge.com

More than 20 frothing rapids are found in this world-beating fissure

23 Summer Solstice

Sydney Observatory, Australia

In the southern hemisphere, the summer solstice is around the 21st-23rd December when the sun is in the sky for around 14.5 hours. Learn dozens of solar system facts at the Sydney Observatory at the top of Observatory Hill.

23 21st – 23rd Dec

❶ Sydney Observatory www.sydneyobservatory.com.au
Sydney Tourism www.sydneyaustralia.com

24 Christmas Eve

Lapland, Finland

According to Finnish legend, Father Christmas resides at Korvatunturi in Urho Kekkonen National Park, on the border of Finland and Russia. Korvantunturi sits on a three-peaked mountain (tunturi) barely 490 m (1,607 ft) high. Children are told that the mountain is hollow and therefore the secret hideaway of Father Christmas, a store of presents, elves, a sleigh and reindeer. As perpetuated by national radio show Markus-sedän lastentunti ("Children's hour with Uncle Markus") hosted by Markus Rautio from 1927-1956, Santa Claus can also hear every word that each child utters – a reason how he knows which children have been bad and which have been good. A few days before the 24th beautifully decorated fir trees are erected and families place grain, nuts and seeds outside for the birds. At the first sight of a twinkling star, candles are lit, saunas taken and fresh, clean clothes put on before a Christmas dinner of roasted ham, salted cod and vegetables at around 6pm. Gifts are exchanged after the final course. The morning of Christmas Day (25th) is a popular time to meet up with neighbours and relatives. Many Finns make a pilgrimage to Korvatunturi although a yuletide arctic theme park close by serves as the modern-day commercial focus.

Christmas Eve in Lapland is a childhood dream all over the world

24 Dec 24th

❶ Korvatunturi Tourism www.korvatunturi.fi
Santa Claus Finland www.santaclaus.fi
Finland Tourism www.visitfinland.com

25 Christmas Day

Marshall Islands

Since the arrival of American missionaries in the 1850's, the Marshall Islands have celebrated Christmas with a mixture of Christian festivities and pagan rituals. From autumn, church groups on each island start working on new compositions and accompanying dances with a Christmas theme. On December 25th, following morning service, the songsters line up outside the Protestant and Assembly of God churches, launching into song and the uniquely Marshallese dance. Bystanders shower the singers with goodies – from cookies and candies to dried foodstuffs, pencils, pens and plastic cups – while the energetic jig dubbed the 'beat' is clapped into a marching procession.

📅 Dec 25th (after Church)

ℹ Marshall Island Tourism www.visitmarshallislands.com

Here Christmas Day is a traditional time to dance the 'beat'

26 Hunt the Wren

Isle of Man, United Kingdom

In the Isle of Man, an age-old Celtic Boxing Day (St Stephen's Day) custom requires rummaging through the hedgerows to find a wren. The annual hunt was once celebrated by Druids when wrens were thought unlucky. Today, a fake bird has replaced the live wren – and it is hidden, rather than chased and involves girls and adults, not just boys. One the wren has been found, it is placed on a decorated pole. Strawboys (or Wrenboys) then dance around it to Celtic music, wearing colourful masks and straw suits.

📅 Dec 26th (Boxing Day)

ℹ Isle of Man Tourism www.gov.im/tourism

27 Sahara Douz Festival | AFRICA

Tunisia

Douz, the largest of Tunisia's oases, 600 km (373 miles) south of Tunis, is venue for the Sahara Douz Festival. Men on Arab stallions draped in gilded cloth open the festivities in a display of fine horsemanship followed by camel races and gun-firing equestrian military parades. Once a simple Bedouin marriage market, the Douz Festival attracts over 55,000 people from all over North Africa.

📅 3 days, late Dec
ⓘ Festival de Douz www.festivaldouz.org.tn

Arab stallions draped in gilded cloth typify displays of horsemanship

28 Harrods' Winter Sale | EUROPE

London, England

The annual post-Christmas sale at London's most prestigious store attracts hardcore shoppers, many of whom camp out for days in front of the main door to take advantage of the bargains. Harrods' grand Winter Sale opening at 9 am on 27th December prompts a surge to the front of the queue. Harrods opened in 1849 and quickly established a reputation for luxury. Over £1 million an hour is spent during the four-week sale on everything from furniture to gourmet food .

📅 Dec 28th
ⓘ Harrods www.harrods.com

29 Crossing of the Cattle | AFRICA

Mali

Herding their cattle safely across the Sahel is a rite of passage for the young Fulani men of Mopti. Custom dictates that they spend a year away from home with their cattle. The Deegal (Crossing Cattle Festival) welcomes them home with food, song and dance. As the festivites continue, the Fulani men share their travel tales with the village and their status and marriage eligibility are assessed by friends, family, neighbours and prospective wives.

📅 Late Dec - early Jan
ⓘ Mali Tourism www.tourisme.gov.ml

30 Deserted Islands | AUSTRALIA/PACIFIC

Aitutaki, Cook Islands

As an alternative to New Year revelry, the Cook Islands provide a chilled out, tranquil escape. About 3,015 km (1,873 miles) northeast of Auckland, the Cooks' nearest neighbours are Tahiti to the east and American Samoa to the west – roughly 1,500 km (932 miles) away. Boasting some of the most unspoiled soft-sand beaches in the region, the isle of Aitutaki sits on a dazzling turquoise-green lagoon dotted with tiny islets (motu). Rich in marine life, Aitutaki attracts a laid-back breed of traveller. On the tiny uninhabited atolls, discover true Robinson Crusoe getaways, where pocket-sized white beaches fringed by coconut palms invoke *Lost World* clichés.

📅 30 Dec for a chilled-out build-up to New Year's Eve

ℹ️ Aitutaki Island Tourism www.aitutaki.com
Cook Islands Tourism www.cook-islands.com

31 Hogmanay | EUROPE

Edinburgh, Scotland

The Scots have always made New Year's Eve (Hogmanay) a celebration to remember – a legacy of Christmas celebrations once having being banned. Until the 1950s, Hogmanay was Scotland's major festival with Christmas a normal working day. Today, Hogmanay remains a highlight of the year running from noon on the 31st December to noon on the 2nd January. Edinburgh, the Scottish capital, plays host to the biggest New Year's Eve party in Europe: a legendary four-day event that begins with a torchlight procession and fire festival on the 29th with a free outdoor Ceilidh (traditional Celtic party) on the 30th. On the 31st, street parties fill the city together with music, concerts and dancing. January 1st is a family day with the 2nd a much-need day of recovery.

📅 31st Dec (over a 3 day public holiday)

ℹ️ Edinburgh Hogmanay www.edinburghshogmanay.org

Scotland's Hogmanay is an exuberant fun-filled affair

Adventure Films: p161; Alexander Agapov: p137; Alexander Fortelny/iStockphoto: p172t; Alexander Khromtsov/ iStockphoto: p91t; Alexander Stark: p70; Alfredas Pliadis (Lithuanian Ministry of National Defence): p103; Alison Wright/ Corbis: p200; Anatoliy Babiychuk/iStockphoto: p202; Andrea De Silva/epa/Corbis: p17; Andy Nelson: p142b; Andy Newman/ Florida Keys News Bureau/HO: p 126, p181; Anna Janeczko: p79; Anne Greenwood/iStockphoto: p187; Anthony Dodd: p174; Ariadne Van Zandbergen/Alamy: p167; aucklandcity.govt.nz: p53; Augusto Motta: p22b; Auke Holwerda/Istockphoto: p66; Bela Szandelszky: p116, p117; Ben Nilsson/Big Ben Productions: p215, p206, p207; Ben Salter: p156; Beren Patterson/Alamy: p185t; Bernhard Richter/ iStockphoto: p108; Bill Keogh/Florida Keys News Bureau/HO: p123; Bill Strange: p127b; Bronsacoerta: p102; C. Lyttle/zefa/ Corbis: p148; CAMRA: p139; Carlos Díaz: p37; Che Kothari: p30; Cheryl Quigley/Istockphoto: p83; Chris Lobina/ Alamy: p39; Chris McLennan/Alamy: p26, p27; Christine Osborne Pictures/Alamy: p59t; Christoph Wilhelm/Getty: p31; compass.krakow.pl: p95; Cuboimages: p59b; Damir Spanic/ iStockphoto: p197; Daniel Kelly: p109; David Cannon/Getty: p141; David Crossland/Alamy: p110; David T Gomez/ iStockphoto: p88; Dennis S. Hurd: p182; Doug Berry/ iStockphoto: p48; Doug Cannell/iStockphoto: p158; Edzard de Ranitz/iStockphoto: p164b; Eli Coory/Fotolia: p28; Emilia Tjernström: p124; Emirates: p92; EmmePi Images/Alamy: p56; eROMAZe/iStockphoto: p186; Eyebyte / Alamy: p119; Fiji Tourism: p120b; Finni Finnbjörnsson/Scubaiceland: p177; Fiona Thomson/www.faithmonsoon.com: p198; Friedrich Stark/ Alamy p32, p33; friendshipfest.com: p84; Fundación Festival de la Leyenda Vallenata: p76; Galen Rowell/Corbis: p94b; Gallway Oyster Festival: p166; gaylord4581: p162; George Steinmetz/ Corbis: p10; Global Eyes: p12; Grand Canyon Skywalk: p65; Greenland Tourism Photo Service: p57, p115; Hazel Dobb: p125t; Heinz Plenge Pardo/Promperu: p86; Hemis/Alamy: p89t; Henley Royal Regatta: p118; Henri Faure/iStockphoto: p91b; Hölland.com: p94t, p136; Homer Sykes/Corbis: p112; Howard: p192; iStockphoto: p212, p210t; J Schmidt: p87; James Lawrence: p127t; Jamjars: p138; Janusz Gniadek/Alamy: p204; Jason Bryant: p98, p99, p114; JNTO: p51, p130t; John Henshall/ Alamy: p218; Jorma Jaemsen/zefa/Corbis: p219; Julia Gomez: p62, p63; Kerim Okten/epa/Corbis: p213; KHAM/Reuters/ Corbis: p74; Kieran Doherty/Reuters/Corbis: p24; Lawrence Cruciana/Fotolia: p16; Leenda Keagle: p190b; Lindsay Hebberd/ Corbis: p155; LOOK Die Bildagentur der Fotografen GmbH/ Alamy: p36; Lovrencg/Fotolia: p41; M Shields Photos/Alamy: p77; Malak: p85b; Mario Vulpis: p85t; Martin Heigan: p196; Max Orchard: p183; Mike King/Corbis: p73; Mustafa Ozer/Getty: p122; NASA: p71; Narinder Nanu/Stringer/AFP: p173; National Maritime Museum, London: p43; Nature Picture Library/Alamy: p185b; Nicolas Leroy: p159t; NL Department of Tourism: p150; Noelii: p145t; Ozimages/Alamy: p168; Paso Robles Main Street Association: p146; Patrick Ward/Alamy: p221; Paul A. Souders/ Corbis: p19; Paul Hahn: p194; Pepa Martín: p89b; Per Helge Rise: p145b; Peter Gorges: p105; Peter Parks/AFP/Getty Images: p144; Peter Pasman: p50; Photogenix/Alamy: p143; Remi Benali/Corbis: p60; Reuters/Corbis: p55, p133t, p130b; Rhoberazzi/iStockphoto: p111; Richard Cummins/Corbis: p190t; Rodd Halstead: p104; Roger Walch: p34; Roman Krochuk/ iStockphoto: p188, p189; Royal College of Art: p203; Sam Hussain: p96; Sampo Tours: p191; sanctuaryretreats.com: p52; Saso Novoselic/Istockphoto: p157; SCPhotos/Alamy: p192b; Seapics: p11, p18, p49b, p101, p211; Sebastian Schreiber: 172b; Sena Vidanagama/Stringer/Getty: p142t; Serban Cristea: p147; Shawn Benjamin Photography incorporating Ark Images: p69; Simon Abrams: p22t; Simon Podgorsek/iStockphoto: p68; Ski Dubai: p151; SNG/Dietz: p210b; Sol Neelman/Corbis: p121; St Andrews Links Trust: p75; State of Vermont: p159b; Stefan Böttcher: p169; Steve Hanna: p180; Steve Razzetti: p80, p81; Stoned59: p149; Stuart Westmorland/Corbis: p179; Suzanne Porter/Alamy: p152, p153; Sven Martin/Cape Epic: p61; Swiatek Wojtkowiak: p93; Tamir Niv/Istockphoto: p165; Tatiana Mironenko/Fotolia: p67; Thomas Sarradet/iStockphoto: p82; Tochigi Prefectyrak Tourism Association Tokyo Office/JNTO: p175; Tod Ragsdale: p164t; Tommaso Granchi: p133b; Tony Marsh: p222; Tony Waltham/Robert Harding World Imagery/ Corbis: p44, p45, p49t; Travel Pix/Alamy: p220; travelwisconsin.com: p125b; Tugu Hotels: p178; Vandan Desai: p8, p9, p17; Vince Millett: p107; Visit Finland: p120t; Vivek Sharma/Alamy: p170, p171; Vulnificans/Fotolia: p42; Whitstable Oyster Festival: p128; WienTourismus/MAXUM: p209; Wildfoods Festival: p54; Winter Marathon: p15; worldconkerchampionships.com: p176; Yasufumi Nishi/JNTO: p29; Yuichi Shiraishi: p162; Zoe McMahon: p47

First published in 2009 by New Holland Publishers (UK) Ltd
London • Cape Town • Sydney • Auckland

www.newhollandpublishers.com

Garfield House, 86-88 Edgware Road, London W2 2EA, UK
80 McKenzie Street, Cape Town 8001, South Africa
Unit 1, 66 Gibbes Street, Chatswood, New South Wales, Australia 2067
218 Lake Road, Northcote, Auckland, New Zealand

10 9 8 7 6 5 4 3 2 1

ISBN 978 1 84773 540 9

Commissioning Editor: Ross Hilton
Design: Paul Wright
Production: Marion Storz
Editorial Direction: Rosemary Wilkinson

Reproduction by Modern Age Repro House Ltd, Hong Kong
Printed and bound in Tien Wah Press (Pte) Ltd, Singapore

Disclaimer
The publisher has made every effort to ensure that the dates and timings in
this book are accurate at the time of going to press. However, dates of
festivals and events do regularly change so you should always check with the
organizers or local authorities before making travel arrangements.